Soul

*Trans-*action Books

Soul

Edited by
LEE RAINWATER

Trans-**action** Books

Published and distributed by
Aldine Publishing Company

The essays in this book originally appeared
in *Trans*-**action** Magazine

TA Book-6
Library of Congress Catalog Number: 76-96129

Contents

Preface

However diverse their attitudes and interpretations may sometimes be, social scientists are now entering a period of shared realization that the United States—both at home and abroad—has entered a crucial period of transition. Indeed, the much burdened word "crisis" has now become a commonplace among black militants, Wall Street lawyers, housewives, and even professional politicians.

For the past six years, *Trans*-action magazine has dedicated itself to the task of reporting the strains and conflicts within the American system. But the magazine has done more than this. It has pioneered in social programs for changing the society, offered the kind of analysis that has permanently restructured the terms of the "dialogue" between peoples and publics, and offered the sort of prognosis that makes for real alterations in social and political policies directly affecting our lives.

The work done in the pages of *Trans*-action has crossed

disciplinary boundaries. This represents much more than simple cross-disciplinary "team efforts." It embodies rather a recognition that the social world cannot be easily carved into neat academic disciplines. That, indeed, the study of the experience of blacks in American ghettos, or the manifold uses and abuses of agencies of law enforcement, or the sorts of overseas policies that lead to the celebration of some dictatorships and the condemnation of others, can best be examined from many viewpoints and from the vantage points of many disciplines.

This series of books clearly demonstrates the superiority of starting with real world problems and searching out practical solutions, over the zealous guardianship of professional boundaries. Indeed, it is precisely this approach that has elicited enthusiastic support from leading American social scientists for this new and dynamic series of books.

The demands upon scholarship and scientific judgment are particularly stringent, for no one has been untouched by the current situation. Each essay republished in these volumes bears the imprint of the author's attempt to communicate his own experience of the crisis. Yet, despite the sense of urgency these papers exhibit, the editors feel that many have withstood the test of time, and match in durable interest the best of available social science literature. This collection of *Trans*-action articles, then, attempts to address itself to immediate issues without violating the basic insights derived from the classical literature in the various fields of social science.

The subject matter of these books concerns social changes that have aroused the long-standing needs and present-day anxieties of us all. These changes are in organizational life styles, concepts of human ability and intelligence, changing patterns of norms and morals, the relationship of social conditions to physical and biological environments, and in the status of social science with national policy making.

This has been a decade of dissident minorities, massive shifts in norms of social conduct, population explosions and urban expansions, and vast realignments between nations of the world. The social scientists involved as editors and authors of this *Trans*-action series have gone beyond observation of these critical areas, and have entered into the vital and difficult tasks of explanation and interpretation. They have defined issues in a way making solutions possible. They have provided answers as well as asked the right questions. Thus, this series should be conceived as the first collection dedicated not to the highlighting of social problems alone, but to establishing guidelines for social solutions based on the social sciences.

THE EDITORS
Trans-action

Introduction

LEE RAINWATER

The decade of the 1960's marked a rediscovery of the Negro American by scholars and the "informed public." Not since the abolitionist-slavery debate of the previous century had there been such an outpouring of scholarly and popular writing concerned with the nation's peculiar institutions for dealing with black men. White America has always tried to make sense out of the Negro, and out of its own guilt-ridden ways of dealing with him. As a scholarly concern, this effort has seen wide swings in its popularity. Not since the last century have intellectual efforts in this area received such wide interest and concern, not since pre-Civil War days has there been the same sense of moral crisis and not since then the same effort to rationally inform the moral impulse.

The images that dominated white intellectual concern with the Negro at the beginning of the decade were those of the bankrupt Southern Jim Crow system and its oppressed Negroes. The images of Negro persons were of the heroic, quietly insistent, "nonviolent" youth who turned the sit-in and the boycott into major techniques of social revolution, and of passive Negro victims whose lives that small group would improve. By the end of the decade, the images that dominated white intellectuals' apprehension of the Negro were very different, revolving around the puzzling, apocalyptic, violent, seemingly other- and self-destructive black man in the central cities.

In the early 1960's when public attention was fixed on the South, "informed people" were increasingly concerned with the situation of Negroes in Northern cities. The Establishment was beginning to focus on what we now know as "the urban crisis" but which then appeared in a variety of guises, most particularly as the problems of juvenile delinquency, of ineffective social services, of de facto school segregation, of the "hard-to-reach," of the "multi-problem family," and finally, of poverty. Every time local and national establishments looked at the city and its troubles they saw black people. Typically, the desire was to understand *them,* since *they* seemed to be at the heart of all these problems.

During the same time, the less-established white elite, particularly the young men and women who had participated directly or vicariously in Southern civil rights activity again turned their attention to home, to their own communities in the North. As they looked around them, they began to understand that however racism had manifested itself down there, the Northern and Western Negro seemed also imprisoned in his ghetto. Out of this combination of Establishment concern, backed by its money (foundation and government) and its ability to focus policy discussion in the nation, and the liberals' and radicals' shock at discovering the South in the North, there came in the middle

1960's a sharp research focus on the black man in "the promised land," to use Claude Brown's devastating phrase.

Beginning with foundation- and government-supported juvenile delinquency research in the late 1950's and continuing on into the sixties with research ostensibly directed toward problems of welfare, housing, the hard-core unemployed and poverty, a large number of sociologists and a very few anthropologists began to take a close look at the Northern ghetto, using primarily the techniques of participant observation and detailed conversational interviewing. This book presents aspects of the work of six of the men who were carrying out such research during the mid-sixties, along with an analysis of some of the issues their work raises by one sociological theorist (Berger) who interprets some of the work on black culture in the context of the society's general stratification system. This volume does not present the wide range of findings represented by the work of these men, or of such others as Kenneth Clark, Hylan Lewis, Elliott Liebow, Charles Valentine, Herbert J. Gans, S. M. Miller and Frank Reisman, whose work taken together repairs the void of empirical study of contemporary race relations that appeared in the post-Myrdal period and that lasted from the late 1940's into the 1960's.

The sociological and anthropological work of the 1960's on the problems of Negro Americans represents to a large extent an updating and modernizing of the earlier work of scholars such as DuBois, Frazier, Edwards, Myrdal, Rose, Davis, Cayton and Drake. But there is in addition a subtle difference between their work and the work of the 1930's and 40's, and this difference may represent a crucial advance over the knowledge developed in the latter period. Earlier studies of Negro social life and personality had emphasized the extent to which Negro behavior could be seen as a direct effect of the caste system maintained by whites. The Negro was presented as a passive product of white-dominated racist institutions. The additions of psychodynamic insights to earlier sociologcal work by such authors as Kardiner and Ovesey and Rohrer and Edmunson deepened that impression.

Black intellectuals who knew and lived the Negro existence were always uneasy with this kind of formulation. On the one hand it was gratifying that white scholars sought to demonstrate that responsibility for the disadvantages Negroes suffer lay squarely upon the white caste; on the other hand the image of Negroes as merely reacting passively to racial oppression seemed to deny them an essential humanity. As in many other ways Ralph Ellison captured the issue quite simply when he asked, "But can a people . . . live and develop for over three hundred years by simply *reacting?* Are American Negroes simply the creation of white men, or have they at least helped create themselves out of what they found around them? Men have made a life in caves and upon cliffs, why cannot Negroes have made a life upon the horns of the white man's dilemma?"

One theme that runs through a great deal of scholarly work on Negro American life in the sixties is exactly that: How black people make a life for themselves on the horns of the white man's dilemma. Social scientists discovered as they looked closely at ghetto lives that they could not provide a valid account of that life without paying much more attention to the creative ways in which Negroes adapted to the situation in which racial oppression placed them. In my own work I have argued that just as the deprivations and depredations practiced by white society have had their effect on the personalities and social life of Negroes, so also has the separation from the ongoing social life of the white community had its effect. In a curious way, Negroes have had more freedom than previously imagined to fashion their own adaptations within their separate world. The larger society provides the black community with few resources but also rarely interferes *on matters that do not seem to affect white interests.* Because Negroes, so also has the separation from the ongoing social they could not depend upon whites to provide they developed their own solutions to recurrent human problems. These solutions can often be seen to combine, along with the predominance of elements from white culture, elements that are distinctive to the Negro group. Even more distinctive is the *configuration* which emerges from those elements Negroes share with whites and those which are different.

It is in this sense that we may speak of a Negro subculture, a distinctive *patterning* of existential perspectives, techniques for coping with the problems of social life, views about what is desirable and undesirable in particular situations. This subculture, and particularly that of the lower-class, the slum Negro, can be seen as his own creation from the elements available to him in response to, first, the conditions of life set by white society and, second, the selective freedom which that society allows (or must put up with, given the pattern of separateness on which it insists).

The most important thing about the freedom that whites have allowed Negroes within their own world is that it has required them to work out their own ways of making it from day to day, from birth to death. The subculture that Negroes have created may be imperfect but it has been viable for centuries; it behooves both white and Negro leaders and intellectuals to seek to understand it even as they hope to see it change.

Negroes have created, again particularly within the lower-class slum group, a range of institutions to structure the tasks of living a victimized life and to minimize the pain it inevitably produces. Prominent among these institutions are those of the nuclear family, the social network —the extended kinship system and "street system" of buddies and girls which tie (although tenuously and unpredictably) the "members" to each other—and the institutions of entertainment (music, dance, folk tales) by which they instruct, explain, and accept themselves. Other institutions function to provide escape from the society of the victimized: the church (Hereafter) and the black freedom movement (Now).

To repeat, some earlier scholars had emphasized the extent to which Negro behavior is an effect of the currently operating caste system, others the extent to which the previous history of slavery and Jim Crow had created a ghetto culture which kept the black man in his place. In both cases, however, the perspective involved an implicit assumption of the Negro's passive response to his situation.

The research of the sixties suggests instead a view of the lower-class Negro subculture as acquiring *limited functional autonomy* from conventional culture and of the social life of the Negro lower class as having a kind of limited functional autonomy vis-à-vis the rest of society. As Gouldner has observed, the phenomenon of functional autonomy in social systems arises in situations where the demands of full functional integration are too great for the resources available in the system. A compromise solution is for subunits of the system to pull apart, to survive more on their own since they cannot survive together in the one big happy family of a functionally integrated system.

This functional autonomy of the lower-class Negro subculture is in the interest of both the larger society and of the group itself. The ghetto requires breathing-room free from the oppressive eye of conventional society, and therefore from the oppressive application of conventional norms. Conventional society is freed from the necessity to face up to the pain and suffering that it has wrought; conventional culture is relieved of the necessity to confront the fact that in the ghetto its norms are constantly flaunted and that the social control mechanisms that are supposed to insure observance cannot operate effectively.

The ghetto subculture, then, can be regarded as the historical creation of persons who are disinherited by their society, persons who have adapted to the twin realities of disinheritance and limited functional autonomy for their group by developing existential perspectives on social reality (including the norms and practices of the larger society) that allow them to stay alive and not lose their minds, that allow them some modicum of hope about a reasonably gratifying life, and that preserve for many the slim hope that somehow they may be able to find admittance for themselves or their children to the larger society. In line with these existential perspectives, the ghetto culture has developed as the repository of a set of survival techniques for functioning in the world of the disinherited.

Discussions of ghetto culture in isolation from the social, economic and ecological setting to which that culture is an adaptation will generally prove to be misleading (and, with respect to policy, pernicious). The dynamic adaptational quality of any culture must be at the center of attention if social process and social change are to be understood. In the case of planned social change directed to solving problems of the ghetto, this means that an appreciation of its culture as an element of ghetto life requires *pari passu* a systematic examination of the day-in-day-out social situation for which that culture provides the tools for folk understanding, evaluation and adaptation.

The articles in this book make amply clear that the ghetto world is defined by two tough facts of life as it is experienced from day to day and from birth to death. These are the facts of deprivation and of exclusion: the ghetto dweller is deprived because he is excluded from the ordinary run of average American working- and middle-class life, and he is excluded because he is deprived of the resources necessary to function in the institutions of mainstream (which is after all working-class, not middle-class) American life.

As the predominantly white sociologists and anthropologists studied social life in the ghettos (the authors represented in this book worked in Washington, Chicago, Oakland, and Los Angeles) during the sixties, one aspect of creative ghetto adaptations which impressed them was the style that black men developed for operating in their world. Elsewhere I have called this the expressive life style, but the late 1960's have produced a more embracing concept under which the expressive style is subsumed—that of soul. The interpersonal styles and their rationales subsumed under the concepts of expressiveness and of soul were neatly presaged for white readers by Ralph Ellison in *Invisible Man*, particularly in the mythic character of Rinehart. Soul could hardly be called a precise conceptual rubric, but as an evocative term it captures nicely both the expressiveness of one characteristic style of Negro adaptation, and the situation to which it is adapted—that of economic and political marginality. The simultaneous importance of situation and adaptation in the idea of soul is well captured in a comment by bluesman Al Hibbler quoted by Charles Keil, who introduced soul as a serious concept in scholarly discussions of Negro life. Speaking of the credentials for becoming a soul singer Hibbler listed in order of importance: having been hurt by a woman, being "brought up in that old time religion," and knowing "what that slavery shit is all about."

The focus on soul concepts, on expressiveness and the street life which is its most appropriate context, involves also a focus by researchers on ghetto men rather than on the women and children who have been the focus of much earlier research. This focus perfectly mirrored, and was perhaps also stimulated by, the shift from primarily passive images of Negroes that were congenial to traditional Southern-oriented race studies to more aggressive images congenial to studies in the big Northern cities particularly as, one by one, they were struck by ghetto riots. However, no sooner had the focus shifted to men and the distinctive ghetto adaptation called soul come in focus, than an argument developed as to what these distinctive adaptations "really meant."

Were they sick or healthy? Were they manifestations of Mertonian retreatism or were they the harbingers of an effective militancy in which Negro men could really get it together? Was soul, in short, an adaptive failure or an heroic adaptation that provided a deep folk resource for the transformation of the ghetto community? Similarly, questions were raised as to whether these soul forms were basically epiphenominal or essential; whether they represented merely a slight variant on the lower-class subculture, the culture of poverty, which could be discovered anywhere that men in the industrial age were unsuccessful in competition for jobs and income, or whether they were the creations of black men out of their distinctive cultural heritage that started in Africa, and was modified by the adaptation to slavery and subsequent white internal colonialism.

The papers in this volume do not really answer all of

these questions, though they raise many of them and make some answers more plausible than others. The papers do, however, go a long way toward providing the reader with an analytic framework within which to consider these issues. The empirical richness of the papers does much to counter the oversimplification of intellectual rhetoric about the ghetto and they focus one's attention sharply on the human issues of how men adapt from day to day and from year to year.

And in the process these papers provide some of the best vignettes of ordinary urban social life in existence. Along with the work of such writers as Elliott Liebow and Claude Brown, they tell us something about urban social life that is significant above and beyond the particular class and race situation of the people studied, much as an ethnically grounded novel, when it is insightful and creative, illuminates the human condition far beyond the ambit of a particular group. (That so much of humanly illuminating sociological and anthropological writing should be about lower-class life raises a curious question. Why is it social scientists seem to be able to find human meaningfulness only in those situations, and are so unsuccessful in capturing it when they study the lives of people who work and live within the working- and middle-class mainstream?)

The papers that follow are interrelated in many ways. Together they serve to define the concept of soul, describe the context within which expressiveness operates in the contemporary ghetto, and raise important conceptual and policy questions about the future of black people. For all their superficially estoteric emphasis on soul, language, rhetoric, music, food and gaming, they show us a great deal about what it is like to be a black man in the space age. The men whose world is described in these papers would probably agree heartily today with the following comment of an eloquent young man of the St. Louis ghetto in 1965.

"You're trying to get to the moon now. There's people in the United States suffering. I mean suffering. Not only white and colored, everybody here is suffering. Yet they say, 'Send money to CARE, for the needy across the sea.' What about the needy here? What about the people here that need help? You're spending millions of dollars missing the moon. You're not gonna hit it that way, Buddy. Spend a million dollars right in your own states."

The first paper, by Ulf Hannerz, a Swedish anthropologist who spent two years studying a Washington ghetto neighborhood as a staff member of Washington's Center for Applied Linguistics, provides an introduction to the soul concept and discusses the various ways in which soul can operate as an adaptive rhetoric for the ghetto situation. John Horton, whose work was done in Los Angeles, analyzes the context, "the set," as the organized gathering in which soul is expressed. He shows how the possibilities inherent in that set shape the adaptations of young men as they grow up and learn to live in the ghetto. Horton's work is an excellent example of the growing ability of sociologists to master traditionally anthropological field methods and to tailor them to the requirements of an urban research site.

Thomas Kochman, a linguist by training and interest, analyzes different kinds of ghetto talk and demonstrates that there exists within the universe of "talking that talk," a high degree of discrimination among different verbal styles depending upon the goal toward which the action is directed. He shows that ghetto talk is not merely colorful or amusing, but that it is sharply instrumental for the man operating on the set.

John Howard, who brings to bear the perspective of

sociological analysis of adult socialization, shifts the focus of the volume toward the adaptation of blacks to the larger society. He shows how becoming a Black Muslim involves a rejection of some traditional expressive elements of lower-class ghetto culture while at the same time the Muslims use an expressive rhetoric which certainly finds its historical roots in that same culture. David Wellman presents a case history of a different kind of adaptation to white society, here represented by the intervention of a war on poverty employment program. A sensitive participant observer and an astute critic of the "opportunities" offered by this particular poverty program, Wellman shows how black youth use ghetto styles to extract what resources out of the program they can, once they discover that in fact it cannot provide them with decent paying jobs.

The last three papers consider the broader issues raised by social and anthropological research on ghetto life styles. Bennett Berger uses Keil's *Urban Blues* as a starting point for taking a critical look at black culture arguments in the context of sociological stratification theory and substantive knowledge concerning the American social structure. He raises in a sharp and clearcut way the question of whether black culture is a phenomenon of race or class, and correlatively, whether it is most properly considered an autonomous creation or a tailored lower-class adaptation. Robert Blauner, who with David Wellman has been studying problems of culture and manhood among blacks and others for several years, addresses this same issue of the meaning of black culture, and responds to Berger from a perspective that is closely attuned to the current militant ferment of the ghetto.

The final paper by Hannerz represents a synthesis of his own Washington ghetto research and the research of others in an effort to answer some of the polemical issues mentioned above involving the question of whether black lower-class men's adaptations are sick or healthy, represent failure or heroic struggle, simply lower-class culture or black culture in the process of creation. His field experience and his ability to analyze it with detachment, enable him to come as close to a synthesis of the varying stances toward ghetto reality as any social scientist is likely to get in the near future.

Harvard University   *Lee Rainwater*
Cambridge, Massachusetts

The Significance of Soul

ULF HANNERZ

In the black ghettos of the large cities of the northern United States, the last few years have witnessed the emergence of the concept of "soul." For instance, in every riot from Watts to Washington, hastily printed signs were rushed to doors and windows of Negro-owned businesses, all carrying the same message: Soul Brother. These businesses were usually spared. Perhaps this is why the term cropped up in a cartoon during the Washington riots —the cartoon showed a "Soul Brother" sign on the iron fence surrounding the White House.

Recently, while doing field work in a lower-class Negro area in Washington, D.C., I considered soul from the standpoint of its social significance in Negro slums in Northern American cities. The neighborhood's inhabitants share the characteristics of America's lower-class urban poor: a high rate of unemployment; a considerable amount of crime (including juvenile delinquency); and a great

15

many households headed by adult women, while the men are either absent or only temporarily attached to the family.

Of the people at the field site, a minority were born in Washington, D.C. The majority are emigrants from the South, particularly from Virginia, North Carolina, and South Carolina. Apart from conducting field work in this area by means of traditional participant observation, I also paid attention to those impersonal media that are specifically intended for a lower-class Negro audience: radio stations (three in Washington were clearly aimed at Negroes); the recording industry; and stage shows featuring Negro rock and roll artists and comedians. (The phrase "rhythm and blues" used by whites to denote Negro rock and roll is not widely used by the Negroes themselves.) These media have played a prominent part in promoting the vocabulary of soul. On the other hand, both the local Negro press, such as the Washington *Afro-American,* and the national Negro publications, like the monthly *Ebony,* are largely middle-class-oriented and thus of limited value for understanding life in the ghetto.

What, then, is soul? As the concept has come to be used in urban ghettos, it stands for "the essence of Negroness." And, it should be added, this "Negroness" refers to the kind of Negro with which the urban slum-dweller is most familar—people like himself. The question whether a middle-class, white-collar, suburban Negro also has soul is often met with consternation. In fact, soul seems to be a folk conception of the lower-class urban Negro's own "national character." Modes of action, personal attributes, and certain artifacts are given the soul label. In conversations one typically hears statements such as "Man, he got a lot of soul." This appreciative opinion may be given concerning anybody in the ghetto, but more often by younger adults or adolescents about their peers. Soul talk is particularly common among younger men. This sex differentiation in the use of soul may be quite important in understanding the basis of the soul concept.

The choice of the term "soul" for this "Negroness" is in itself noteworthy. First of all, it shows the influence of religion on lower-class Negroes, even those who are not themselves active church members. Expressions of religious derivation—such as "God, have mercy!"—are frequent in everyday speech among all lower-class Negroes, in all contexts. A very great number of people, of course, have been regular churchgoers at some point, at least at the time they attended Sunday school, and many are involved in church activities—perhaps in one of the large Baptist churches, but more often in small spiritualist storefront churches. Although the people who use the soul vocabulary are seldom regular churchgoers themselves, they have certainly been fully (although sometimes indirectly) exposed to the religious idiom of "soul-stirring" revival meetings.

Further, the choice of soul (a term that in church usage means "the essentially human") to refer to "the essentially Negro," as the new concept of soul does, certainly has strong implications of race pride. If soul is Negro, the non-Negro is non-soul, and, in a unique turnabout, somewhat less human. Although I have never heard such a point of view spelled out, it seems to be implicitly accepted as part of soul ideology. What is soul is not only different from what is not soul (particularly what is mainstream, middle-class American); it is also superior. The term "soul" appraises as well as describes. If one asks a young man what a soul brother is, the answer is usually something like "Someone who's hip, someone who knows what he's doing." It may be added here that although both soul brother and soul sister are used for soul personified, the former is more common. Like soul, soul brother and soul sister are terms used particularly by younger men.

Let us now note a few fields that are particularly soulful. One is music (where the concept may have originated), especially progressive jazz and rock and roll. James Brown, a leading rock and roll singer, is often referred to as "Soul Brother Number One"; two of the largest record stores in Washington, with almost exclusively Negro customers, are the "Soul Shack" and the "Soul City." Recently a new magazine named *Soul* appeared; its main outlet seems to be these de facto segregated record stores. It contains stories on rock and roll artists, disc jockeys, and so on. Excellence in musical expression is indeed a part of the lower-class Negro's self-conception, and white rock and roll is often viewed with scorn as a poor imitation of the Negro genius. Resentment is often aimed at the Beatles, who stand as typical of white intrusion into a Negro field. (Occasionally a Beatles melody has become a hit in the Negro ghetto as well, but only when performed in a local version by a Negro group, such as the recording of "Day Tripper" by the Vontastics. In such a case, there is little or no mention of the melody's Beatles origin.)

The commercial side of Negro entertainment is, of course, directly tied to soul music. The Howard Theater in Washington, with counterparts in other large Negro ghettos in the United States, stages shows of touring rock and roll groups and individual performers. Each show usually runs a week, with four or five performances every day. Larger shows also make one-night appearances at the Washington Coliseum. Occasionally, a comedian takes part; Moms Mabley, Pigmeat Markham, and Red Foxx are among those who draw large, predominantly Negro audiences.

The emcees of these shows are often celebrities in their own right. Some, such as "King" Coleman and "Georgeous"

George, tour regularly with the shows, and others are local disc jockeys from the white-owned Negro radio stations. In Washington, such disc jockeys as "The Nighthawk," Bob Terry of the WOL "Soul Brothers," and "Soulfinger," Fred Correy of the WOOK "Soul Men," make highly appreciated appearances at the Howard. It is clear that the commercial establishments with a vested interest in a separate Negro audience have latched onto the soul vocabulary, using it to further their own interests as well to support its use among the audience. Thus there is also, for instance, a WWRL "soul brother radio" in New York. But the soul vocabulary is not just a commercial creation. It existed before it was commercialized, and the fact that it seems so profitable for commercial establishments to fly the banner of soul indicates that, whatever part these establishments have had in promoting soul, it has fallen into already fertile ground.

A second area of widespread soul symbolism is food. The dishes that Negroes now call soul food they once called "Southern cooking" and still do to some extent; but in the Northern ghettos these foods increasingly come to stand for race rather than region. In the center of the Washington Negro area, for instance, the Little Harlem Restaurant advertises "soul food." There are a number of such foods: chitlins, hog maw, black-eyed peas, collard greens, corn bread, and grits. Typically, they were the poor man's food in the rural South. In the urban North, they may still be so to some degree, but in the face of the diversity of the urban environment they also come to stand as signs of ethnicity. References to soul food occur frequently in soul music—two of the hits of the winter 1966-67 were "Grits and Cornbread" by the Soul Runners and the Joe Cuba Sextet's "Bang! Bang!," with the refrain "corn bread, hog maw, and chitlin." Sometimes the names of soul foods may themselves be used as more or less synonymous with soul—Negro entertainers on stage, talking of their experiences while journeying between ghetto shows around the country, sometimes refer to it as "the chitlin circuit," and this figure of speech usually draws much favorable audience reaction.

What, then, is "soul" about soul music and soul food? It may be wise to be cautious here, since there is little intellectualizing and analyzing on the part of the ghetto's inhabitants on this subject. I believe that this comparative absence of defining may itself be significant, and I will return to this later. Here, I will only point to a few basic characteristics of soul that I feel make it "essentially Negro" —referring again, of course, to urban lower-class Negroes.

There is, of course, the Southern origin. The "Down Home" connotations are particularly attached to soul food; but while Negro music has changed more, and commercial rock and roll is an urban phenomenon, this music is certainly seen as the latest stage of an unfolding heritage. Thus the things that are soul, while taking on new significance in the urban environment, provide some common historical tradition for ghetto inhabitants. One might also speculate that the early and, from then on, constant and intimate exposure to these foods and to this music—radios and record players seem to belong to practically every ghetto home—may make them appear particularly basic to a "Negro way of life."

When it comes to soul music, there are a couple of themes in style and content that I would suggest are pervasive in ghetto life, and are probably very close to the everyday experience of ghetto inhabitants.

One of these is lack of control over the environment. There is a very frequent attitude among soul brothers that one's environment is somewhat like a jungle, where tough, smart people may survive and where a lot happens to make it worthwhile and enjoyable just to "watch the scene"—if one does not have too high hopes of controlling it. Many of the reactions to listening to progressive jazz seem connected with this view: "Oooh, man, there just ain't nothing you can do about it but sit there and feel it goin' all the way into you." Without being able to do much about proving it, I feel that experiences—desirable or undesirable —in which one can only passively perceive what is happening are an essential fact of ghetto life, for better or for worse; thus it is soul.

Related to this theme are unstable personal relationships, in particular between the sexes. It is well known that among lower-class urban Negroes there are many "broken" families (households without a husband and father), many temporary common-law unions, and in general relatively little consensus on sex roles. It is not much of an exaggeration, then, to speak of a constant battle of the sexes. Indeed, success with the opposite sex is a focal concern in lower-class Negro life. From this area come most of the lyrics of contemporary rock and roll music. (It may be objected that this is true of white rock and roll as well; but this is very much to the point. For white rock and roll is predominantly adolescent music, and reaches people who also have unstable personal relationships. In the case of lower-class urban Negroes, such relationships are characteristic of a much wider age-range, and music on this theme also reaches this wider range.) Some titles of recent rock and roll hits may show this theme: "I'm Losing You" (Temptations), "Are You Lonely" (Freddy Scott), "Yours Until Tomorrow" (Dee Dee Warwick), "Keep Me Hangin' On" (Supremes). Thus soul may also stand for a bittersweet experience that arises from contacts with the other sex (although there are certainly other sources). This bittersweetness, of course, was already typical of the blues.

Turning to style, a common element in everyday social interaction—as well as among storefront-church preachers, Negro comedians, and rock and roll singers—is an alternation between aggressive, somewhat boastful behavior and plaintive behavior from an implicit underdog position. This style occurs in many situations and may itself be related to the unstable personal relationships mentioned above. In any case, it seems that this style is seen as having soul; without describing its elements, soul brothers tend to describe its occurrences in varying contexts as "soulful."

I have hesitated to try to analyze and define soul, because what seems to be important in the emergence of the present soul concept is the fact that there is *something* that is felt to be soul; *what* that something is isn't so important. There is, of course, some logic to this. If soul is what is "essentially Negro," it should not be necessary for soul brothers to spend much time analyzing it. Asking about soul, one often receives answers such as, "You know, we don't talk much about it, but we've all been through it, so we know what it is anyway." Probably this is to some extent true. What the lack of a clear definition points to is that soul vocabulary is predominantly for the in-crowd. It is a symbol of solidarity among the people of the ghetto —but not in more than a weak and implicit sense of solidarity *against* anybody else. Soul is turned inward; and so everybody who is touched by it is supposed to know what it means.

The few interpreters of soul to the outside world are, in fact, outsiders. LeRoi Jones, the author, is a convert to ghetto life who, like so many converts, seems to have become more militantly partisan than the authentic ghetto inhabitants. Originally he rather impartially noted the ethnocentric bias of soul:

"... the soul brother means to recast the social order

in his own image. White is then not 'right,' as the old blues had it, but a liability, since the culture of white precludes the possession of the Negro 'soul.' "

Now he preaches the complete destruction of American society, an activist program that I am sure is far out of step with the immediate concerns of the average soul brother. Lerone Bennett, an editor of the middle-class *Ebony* magazine, is not particularly interested in what he calls "the folk myth of soul," yet he explains what he feels soul really is:

". . . the American counterpart of the African concept of Negritude, a distinct quality of Negroness growing out of the Negro's experience and not his genes. . . . Soul is the Negro's antithesis to America's thesis (white), a confrontation of spirits that could and should lead to a higher synthesis of the two."

I am not convinced that Bennett's conception is entirely correct; it is certainly not expressed in the idiom of the ghetto. Charles Keil, an ethomusicologist, probably comes closer to the folk conception than anyone else—by giving what amounts to a catalogue of those ghetto values and experiences that the inhabitants recognize as their own:

"The breath of life"; "It don't mean a thing if you ain't got that swing"; "Grits and greens"; and so on.

In doing so, of course, one does not get a short and comprehensive definition of soul that is acceptable to all and in every situation—one merely lists the fields in which a vocabulary of soul is particularly likely to be expressed.

The vocabulary of soul, then, is a relatively recent phenomenon, and it is used among younger Negro ghetto dwellers, particularly young men, to designate in a highly approving manner the experiences and characteristics that are "essentially Negro." As such, it is employed within the group, although it is clear that by discussing what is "typically Negro" one makes an implicit reference to non-Negro society. Now, why has such a vocabulary emerged in this group at just this point of Negro history?

For a long time, the social boundaries that barred Negro Americans from educational and economic achievements have been highly impermeable. Although lower-class Negroes largely accepted the values of mainstream American culture, the obvious impermeability of social boundaries has probably prevented a more complete commitment on their part to the achievement of those goals that have been out of reach. Instead, there has been an adjustment to the lower-class situation, in which goals and values more appropriate to the ascribed social position of the group have been added to, and to some extent substituted for, the mainstream norms. The style of life of the lower class, in this case the Negro lower class, is different from that of the upper classes, and the impermeability of group boundaries and the unequal distribution of resources have long kept the behavioral characteristics of the groups relatively stable and distinct from each other. However, to a great extent, one of the groups—the lower-class Negroes—would have preferred the style of life of the other group—the middle-class whites—had it been available to them.

Lower-class Negroes have only been able to do the best they could with what they have had. They have had two cultures—the mainstream culture they are relatively familiar with, which is in many ways apparently superior and preferable and which has been closed to them, and the ghetto culture, which is a second choice and is based on the circumstances of the ascribed social position.

This, of course, sounds to some extent like the position of what has often been described as that of "the marginal man." Such a position may cause psychological problems. But when the position is very clearly defined and where the same situation is shared by many, it is perhaps reasonably acceptable. There is a perfectly understandable reason for one's failure to reach one's goal. Nobody of one's own kind is allowed to reach that goal, and the basis of the condition is a social rule rather than a personal failure. There are indications that marginality is more severely felt if the barrier is not absolute—if crossing a boundary, although uncertain, is possible. According to Alan C. Kerckhoff and Thomas C. McCormick,

"... an absolute barrier between the two groups is less conducive to personality problems than 'grudging, uncertain, and unpredictable acceptance.' The impact of the rejection on an individual's personality organization will depend to some extent upon the usual treatment accorded members of his group by the dominant group. If his group as a whole faces a rather permeable barrier and he meets with more serious rejection, the effect on him is likely to be more severe than the same treatment received by a more thoroughly rejected group (one facing an impermeable barrier)."

Recent changes in race relations in the United States have indeed made the social barriers to achievement seem less impermeable to the ghetto population. One often hears people in the ghetto expressing opinions such as, "Yeah, there are so many programs, job-training and things, going on, man, so if you got anything on the ball you can make it." On the other hand, there are also assertions about the impossibility of getting anywhere. Obviously, a clear-cut exclusion from mainstream American culture is gradually being replaced by ambivalence about one's actual chances. This ambivalence, of course, seems to represent an accurate estimate of the situation: The lower-class Negro continues to be disadvantaged, but his chances of moving up and out of the ghetto are probably improving.

People do indeed trickle out of the ghetto.

It is in this situation that the vocabulary of soul has emerged. It is a response, I feel, to the uncertainty of the ghetto dweller's situation. This uncertainty is particularly strong for the younger male, the soul brother. While women have always been able to live closer to mainstream culture norms, as homemakers and possibly with a job keeping them in touch with the middle-class world, men have had less chance to practice and become competent in mainstream culture. Older men tend to feel that current social changes come too late for them, but they have higher expectations for the following generation. Therefore, the present generation of young men in the Negro ghettos of the United States is placed in a new situation, to which they are making new responses, and much of the unrest in the ghettos today is perhaps the result of these emerging pressures.

This new situation must be taken into account if we are to understand the emergence of the soul vocabulary. The increasing ambivalence about one's opportunities in the changing social structure may be accompanied by doubts about one's own worth. Earlier, the gap between mainstream culture norms and the lower-class Negro's achievements could be explained easily, by referring to social barriers. Today, the suspicion arises that under-achievement is due to one's own failure, and self-doubt may result.

Such self-doubt can be reduced in different ways. Some young men, of course, are able to live up to mainstream norms of achievement, thereby reducing the strain on themselves (but at the same time increasing the strain on the others). Higher self-esteem can also be obtained by affirming that the boundaries are still impermeable. A third possibility is to set new standards for achievement, proclaiming one's own achievements to be the ideals. It is not necessary, of course, that the same way of reducing self-doubt always be applied. In the case of soul, the method is that of idealizing one's own achievements, proclaiming one's own way of life to be superior. Yet the same soul brother may argue at other times that he is what he is because he is not allowed to become anything else.

In any case, soul is by native public definition superior, and the motive of the soul vocabulary, I believe, is above all to reduce self-doubt by persuading soul brothers that they are successful. Being a soul brother is belonging to a select group instead of to a residual category of people who have not succeeded. Thus, the soul vocabulary is a device of rhetoric. By talking about people who have soul, about soul music and about soul food, the soul brother attempts to establish himself in the role of an expert and connoisseur; by talking to others of his group in these terms, he identifies with them and confers the same role on them. Using soul rhetoric is a way of convincing others of one's own worth and of their worth. As Kenneth Burke expresses it,

"A man can be his own audience, insofar as he, even in his secret thoughts, cultivates certain ideas or images for the effect he hopes they may have upon him; he is here what Mead would call 'an "I" addressing its "me" '; and in this respect he is being rhetorical quite as though he were using pleasant imagery to influence an outside audience rather than one within."

The soul vocabulary has thus emerged from the social basis of a number of individuals, in effective interaction with one another, with similar problems of adjustment to a new situation. The use of soul rhetoric is a way of meeting their needs as long as it occurs in situations where they can mutually support each other. Here, of course, is a clue to the confinement of the rhetoric to in-group situations.

If soul talk were directed toward outsiders, they might not accept the claims of its excellence—it is not *their* "folk myth." Viewing soul as such a device of rhetoric, it is also easier to understand why the soul brothers do not want it made the topic of too much intellectualizing. As Clifford Geertz has made clear, by analyzing and defining an activity one achieves maximum intellectual clarity at the expense of emotional commitment. It is doubtful that soul rhetoric would thrive on too much intellectual clarity; rather, by expressing soul ideals in a circumspect manner—in terms of emotionally charged symbols such as soul food and soul music—one can avoid the rather sordid realities underlying these emotions. As I pointed out already, the shared lower-class Negro experiences that seem to be the bases of soul are hardly such as to bring out a surge of ethnic pride. That is the psychological reason for keeping the soul concept diffuse.

There is also, I believe, a sociological basis for the diffuseness. The more exactly a soul brother would define soul, the fewer others would probably agree upon the "essential Negroness" of his definition; and, as we have seen, a basic idea of the rhetoric of soul is to cast others into roles that satisfy them and at the same time support one's own position. If people are cast into a role of soul brother and then find that there has been a definition established for that role that they cannot accept, the result may be overt disagreement and denial of solidarity, rather than mutual deference. As it is, soul can be an umbrella concept for a rather wide variety of definitions of one's situation, and the soul brothers who are most in need of the race-centered conception can occasionally get at least fleeting allegiance to soul from others with whom, in reality, they share relatively little—for instance, individuals who are clearly upwardly mobile. Once I listened to a long conversation about soul music in a rather heterogeneous group of young Negro men, who all agreed on the soulfulness of the singers whose records they were playing. Afterwards I asked one of the men, who was clearly upwardly mobile, about his conception of soul. He answered that soul is earthy, that "There is nothing specifically Negro about it." Yet the very individuals with whom he had just agreed on matters of soul had earlier given me the opposite answer—only Negroes have soul. Thus, by avoiding definitions, they had found together an area of agreement and satisfaction in soul by merely assuming that there was a shared basis of opinion.

To sum up: Soul has arisen at this point because of the Negro's increasingly ambivalent conceptions about the opportunity structure. Earlier, lack of achievement according to American mainstream ideals could easily be explained in terms of impermeable social barriers. Now the impression is gaining ground that there are ways out of the situation. The young men who come under particularly great strain if such a belief is accepted must either achieve (which many of them are obviously still unable to do); explain that achievement is impossible (which is probably no longer true); or explain that achievement according to mainstream ideals is not necessarily achievement according to their *own* ideals. The emergence of soul goes some way toward meeting the need of stating alternative ideals, and also provides solidarity among those with such a need. And it is advantageous to maintain a diffuse conception of soul, for if an intellectually clear definition were established, soul would probably be both less convincing and less uniting.

The view of soul taken here is, in short, one of a piecemeal rhetorical attempt to establish a satisfactory self-image. I am sure that, for the great majority of soul brothers, this is the major basis of soul. It may be added that LeRoi Jones and Charles Keil take a more social-activist view of soul, although Keil tends to make it a prophecy rather than an interpretation. At present, I think that there is little basis for their connecting the majority of soul brothers with militant black nationalism. But organized black nationalism may be able to recruit followers by using some kind of transformed soul vocabulary, and I think there are obviously political attempts now under way to make more of soul. Thus, if at present it is not possible to speak of more than a "rhetoric of soul," it may well be that in the future we will have a "soul movement." *too true!*

July/August 1968

Time and Cool People

JOHN HORTON

Time in industrial society is clock time. It seems to be an external, objective regulator of human activities. But for the sociologist, time is not an object existing independent of man, dividing his day into precise units. Time is diverse; it is always social and subjective. A man's sense of time derives from his place in the social structure and his lived experience.

The diversity of time perspectives can be understood intellectually—but it is rarely tolerated socially. A dominant group reifies and objectifies its time; it views all other conceptions of time as subversive—as indeed they are.

Thus, today in the dominant middle-class stereotype, standard American time is directed to the future; it is rational and impersonal. In contrast, time for the lower class is directed to the present, irrational and personal. Peasants, Mexican-Americans, Negroes, Indians, workers are "lazy"; they do not possess the American virtues of ambition and striving for success. Viewed solely from the dominant class norm of rationality, their presumed orientation to present time is seen only as an irrational deviation, something to be controlled and changed. It is at best an epiphenomenon produced in reaction to the "real, objective" phenomenon of middle-class time.

Sociologists have not been completely exempt from this kind of reified thinking. When they universalize the middle-class value of rational action and future time and turn it into a "neutral" social fact, they reinforce a negative stereotype: Lower classes are undependable in organized work situations (they seek immediate rewards and cannot defer gratification); in their political action, they are prone to accept immediate, violent, and extreme solutions to personal problems; their sense of time is dysfunctional to the stability of the economic and political orders. For example, Seymour Martin Lipset writes, in a paper significantly entitled "Working Class Authoritarianism":

This emphasis on the immediately perceivable and concern with the personal and concrete is part and parcel of the short time perspective and the inability to perceive the complex possibilities and consequences of action which often results in a general readiness to support extremist political and religious movements, and generally lower level of liberalism on noneconomic questions.

To examine time in relation to the maintenance or destruction of the dominant social order is an interesting political problem, but it is not a sociology of time; it is a middle-class sociology of order or change in its time aspect. Surely, a meaningful sociology of time should take into account the social situation in which time operates and the actor's as well as the observer's perspective. The sociologist must at least entertain the idea that lower-class time may be a phenomenon in and of itself, and quite functional to the life problems of that class.

Of course, there are dangers in seeking the viewpoint of a minority: The majority stereotypes might be reversed. For example, we might find out that no stereotype is more incorrect than that which depicts the lower classes as having no sense of future time. As Max Weber has observed, it is the powerful and not the powerless who are present-oriented. Dominant groups live by maintaining and expanding their present. Minority groups survive in this present, but their survival is nourished by a dream of the future. In "Ethnic Segregation and Caste" Weber says:

> The sense of dignity that characterizes positively privi-leged status groups is natural to their "being" which does not transcend itself, that is, to their beauty and excellence. Their kingdom is of this world. They live for the present by exploiting the great past. The sense of dignity of the negatively privileged strata naturally refers to a future lying beyond the present whether it is of this life or an-other. In other words it must be nurtured by a belief in a providential "mission" and by a belief in a specific honor before God.

It is time to reexamine the meaning of time, the reality of the middle-class stereotype of itself, as well as the middle-class stereotype of the lower class. In this article I explore the latter: the meaning of time among a group most often stereotyped as having an irrational, present sense of time— the sporadically unemployed young Negro street corner population. I choose the unemployed because they live out-side of the constraints of industrial work time; Negroes because they speak some of the liveliest street language, including that of time; young males because the street culture of the unemployed and the hustler is young and masculine.

To understand the meaning of street time was to discover

"what's happening" in the day-to-day and week-to-week activities of my respondents. Using the middle-class stereotype of lower-class time as a point of departure, I asked myself the following questions:

■ In what sense is street time personal (not run by the clock) and present-oriented?

■ What kind of future orientation, if any, exists?

■ Are street activities really irrational in the sense that individuals do not use time efficiently in the business of living? I have attempted to answer the questions in the language and from the experience of my respondents.

Street culture exists in every low income ghetto. It is shared by the hustling elements of the poor, whatever their nationality or color. In Los Angeles, members of such street groups sometimes call themselves "street people," "cool people," or simply "regulars." Whatever the label, they are known the world over by outsiders as hoods or hoodlums, persons who live on and off the street. They are recognizable by their own fashions in dress, hair, gestures, and speech. The particular fashion varies with time, place, and nationality. For example, in 1963 a really sharp Los Angeles street Negro would be "conked to the bone" (have processed hair) and "togged-out" in "continentals." Today "natural" hair and variations of mod clothes are coming in style.

Street people are known also by their activities—"duking" (fighting or at least looking tough), "hustling" (any way of making money outside the "legitimate" world of work), "gigging" (partying)—and by their apparent nonactivity, "hanging" on the corner. Their individual roles are defined concretely by their success or failure in these activities. One either knows "what's happening" on the street, or he is a "lame," "out of it," "not ready" (lacks his diploma in street knowledge), a "square."

There are, of course, many variations. Negroes, in particular, have contributed much to the street tongue which has diffused into both the more hip areas of the middle class and the broader society. Such expressions as "a lame," "taking care of righteous business," "getting down to the nitty-gritty," and "soul" can be retraced to Negro street life.

The more or less organized center of street life is the "set"—meaning both the peer group and the places where it hangs out. It is the stage and central market place for activity, where to find out what's happening. My set of Negro street types contained a revolving and sometimes disappearing (when the "heat," or police pressure, was on) population of about 45 members ranging in age from 18 to 25. These were the local "dudes," their term meaning not the fancy city slickers but simply "the boys," "fellas," the "cool people." They represented the hard core of street culture, the role models for younger teenagers. The dudes could be found when they were "laying dead"—hanging on the corner, or shooting pool and "jiving" ("goofing" or kidding around) in a local community project. Isolated from "the man" (in this context the man in power—the police, and by extension, the white man), they lived in a small section of Venice outside the central Los Angeles ghetto and were surrounded by a predominantly Mexican and Anglo population. They called their black "turf" "Ghost-town"—home of the "Ghostmen," their former gang. Whatever the origin of the word, Ghost-town was certainly the home of socially "invisible" men.

In 1965 and 1966 I had intensive interviews with 25 set members. My methods emerged in day to day observations. Identified as white, a lame, and square, I had to build up an image of being at least "legit" (not working for police). Without actually living in the area, this would have been impossible without the aid of a key fieldworker, in this case an outsider who could be accepted inside. This field worker, Cowboy, was a white dude of 25. He had run with "Paddy" (white), "Chicano" (Mexican), and "Blood" (Negro) sets since the age of 12 and was highly respected for having been president of a tough gang. He knew the street, how to duke, move with style, and speak the tongue. He made my entry possible. I was the underprivileged child who had to be taught slowly and sympathetically the common-sense features of street life.

Cowboy had the respect and I the toleration of several set leaders. After that, we simply waited for the opportunity to "rap." Although sometimes used synonymously with street conversation, "rap" is really a special way of talking—repartee. Street repartee at its best is a lively way of "running it down," or of "jiving" (attempting to put someone on), of trying "to blow another person's mind," forcing him "to loose his cool," to give in or give up something. For example, one needs to throw a lively rap when he is "putting the make on a broad."

Sometimes we taped individuals, sometimes "soul sessions." We asked for life histories, especially their stories about school, job, and family. We watched and asked about the details of daily surviving and attempted to construct street time schedules. We probed beyond the past and present into the future in two directions—individual plans for tomorrow and a lifetime, and individual dreams of a more decent world for whites and Negroes.

The set can be described by the social and attitudinal characteristics of its members. To the observer, these are expressed in certain realities of day to day living: not enough skill for good jobs, and the inevitable trouble brought by the problem of surviving. Of the 25 interviewed, only four had graduated from high school. Except for a younger set member who was still in school, all were dropouts, or perhaps more accurately kicked-outs. None was really able to use or write formal language. However, many were highly verbal, both facile and effective in their use of the street tongue. Perhaps the art of conversation is most highly developed here where there is much time to talk, perhaps too much—an advantage of the *lumpen*-leisure class.

Their incomes were difficult to estimate, as "bread" or "coins" (money) came in on a very irregular basis. Of the 17 for whom I have figures, half reported that they made less than $1,400 in the last year, and the rest claimed income from $2,000-4,000 annually. Two-thirds were living with and partially dependent on their parents, often a mother. The financial strain was intensified by the fact that although 15 of 17 were single, eight had one or more children living in the area. (Having children, legitimate or not, was not a stigma but proof of masculinity.)

At the time of the interview, two-thirds of them had some full- or part-time employment—unskilled and low-paid jobs. The overall pattern was one of sporadic and—from their viewpoint—often unsatisfactory work, followed by a period of unemployment compensation, and petty hustling whenever possible and whenever necessary.

When I asked the question, "When a dude needs bread, how does he get it?" the universal response was "the hustle." Hustling is, of course, illegitimate from society's viewpoint. Street people know it is illegal, but they view it in no way as immoral or wrong. It is justified by the necessity of surviving. As might be expected, the unemployed admitted that they hustled and went so far as to say that a dude could make it better on the street than on the job: "There is a lot of money on the street, and there are many ways of getting it," or simply, "This has always been my way of life." On the other hand, the employed, the part-time hustlers, usually said, "A dude could make it better on the job than on the street." Their reasons for disapproving of hustling were not moral. Hustling meant trouble. "I don't hustle because there's no security. You eventually get busted." Others said there was not enough money on the street or that it was too difficult to "run a game" on people.

Nevertheless, hustling is the central street activity. It is the economic foundation for everyday life. Hustling and the fruit of hustling set the rhythm of social activities.

What are the major forms of hustling in Ghost-town? The best hustles were conning, stealing, gambling, and selling dope. By gambling, these street people meant dice; by dope, peddling "pills" and "pot." Pills are "reds" and "whites"—barbiturates and benzedrine or dexedrine. Pot is, of course, marijuana—"grass" or "weed." To "con" means to put "the bump" on a "cat," to "run a game" on somebody, to work on his mind for goods and services.

The "woman game" was common. As one dude put it, "If I have a good lady and she's on County, there's always some money to get." In fact, there is a local expression for getting county money. When the checks come in for child support, it's "mother's day." So the hustler "burns" people for money, but he also "rips off" goods for money; he thieves, and petty thieving is always a familiar hustle. Pimping is often the hustler's dream of the good life, but it was almost unknown here among the small-time hustlers. That was the game of the real professional and required a higher level of organization and wealth.

Hustling means bread and security but also trouble, and trouble is a major theme in street life. The dudes had a "world of trouble" (a popular song about a hustler is "I'm in a World of Trouble")—with school, jobs, women, and the police. The intensity of street life could be gauged in part by the intensity of the "heat" (police trouble). The hotter the street, the fewer the people visible on the street. On some days the set was empty. One would soon learn that there had been a "bust" (an arrest). Freddy had run amok and thrown rocks at a police car. There had been a leadership struggle; "Big Moe" had been cut up, and the "fuzz" had descended. Life was a succession of being picked up on suspicion of assault, theft, possession, "suspicion of suspicion" (an expression used by a respondent in describing his life). This was an ordinary experience for the street dude and often did lead to serious trouble. Over half of those interviewed claimed they had felony convictions.

Keeping cool and out of trouble, hustling bread, and looking for something interesting and exciting to do created the structure of time on the street. The rhythm of time is expressed in the high and low points in the day and week of an unemployed dude. I stress the pattern of the unemployed and full-time hustler because he is on the street all day and night and is the prototype in my interviews. The sometimes employed will also know the pattern, and he will be able to hit the street whenever released from the bondage of jail, work, and the clock. Here I describe a typical time schedule gleaned through interviews and field observation.

Characteristically the street person gets up late, hits the street in the late morning or early afternoon, and works his way to the set. This is a place for relaxed social activity. Hanging on the set with the boys is the major way of passing time and waiting until some necessary or desirable action occurs. Nevertheless, things do happen on the set. The dudes "rap" and "jive" (talk), gamble, and drink their "pluck" (usually a cheap, sweet wine). They find out what happened yesterday, what is happening today, and what will hopefully happen on the weekend—the perpetual search for the "gig," the party. Here peer socialization and reinforcement also take place. The younger dude feels a sense of pride when he can be on the set and throw a rap to an older dude. He is learning how to handle himself, show respect, take care of business, and establish his own "rep."

On the set, yesterday merges into today, and tomorrow is an emptiness to be filled in through the pursuit of bread and excitement. Bread makes possible the excitement—the high (getting loaded with wine, pills, or pot), the sharp clothes, the "broad," the fight, and all those good things which show that one knows what's happening and has "something going" for himself. The rhythm of time—of the day and of the week—is patterned by the flow of money and people.

Time is "dead" when money is tight, when people are occupied elsewhere—working or in school. Time is dead when one is in jail. One is "doing dead time" when nothing is happening, and he's got nothing going for himself.

Time is alive when and where there is action. It picks up in the evening when everyone moves on the street. During the regular school year it may pick up for an hour in the afternoon when the "broads" leave school and meet with the set at a corner taco joint. Time may pick up when a familiar car cruises by and a few dudes drive down to Johnny's for a "process" (hair straightening and styling). Time is low on Monday (as described in the popular song, "Stormy Monday"), Tuesday, Wednesday, when money is tight. Time is high on Friday nights when the "eagle flies" and the "gig" begins. On the street, time has a personal meaning only when something is happening, and something is most likely to happen at night—especially on Friday and Saturday nights. Then people are together, and there may be bread—bread to take and bread to use.

Human behavior is rational if it helps the individual to get what he wants whether it is success in school or happiness in the street. Street people sometimes get what they want. They act rationally in those situations where they are able to plan and choose because they have control, knowledge, and concern, irrationally where there are barriers to their wants and desires.

When the street dude lacks knowledge and power to manipulate time, he is indeed irrational. For the most part, he lacks the skills and power to plan a move up and out of the ghetto. He is "a lame" in the middle class world of school and work; he is not ready to operate effectively in unfamiliar organizations where his street strengths are his visible weaknesses. Though irrational in moving up and out of the street, he can be rational in day to day survival in the street. No one survives there unless he knows what's happening (that is, unless he knows what is available, where to get what he can without being burned or busted). More euphemistically, this is "taking advantage of opportunities," exactly what the rational member of the middle class does in his own setting.

To know what's happening is to know the goods and the bads, the securities, the opportunities, and the dangers of the street. Survival requires that a hustling dude know who is cool and uncool (who can be trusted) ; who is in power (the people who control narcotics, fences, etc.) ; who is the "duker" or the fighter (someone to be avoided or someone who can provide protection). When one knows what's happening he can operate in many scenes, providing that he can "hold his mud," keep cool, and out of trouble.

With his diploma in street knowledge, a dude can use time efficiently and with cunning in the pursuit of goods and services—in hustling to eat and yet have enough bread left over for the pleasures of pot, the chicks, and the gig. As one respondent put it, "The good hustler has the know-how, the ambition to better himself. He conditions his mind and must never put his guard too far down, to relax, or he'll be taken." This is street rationality. The problem is not a deficient sense of time but deficient knowledge and control to make a fantasy future and a really better life possible.

The petty hustler more fully realizes the middle class ideal of individualistic rationality than does the middle class itself. When rationality operates in hustling, it is often on an individual basis. In a world of complex organization, the hustler defines himself as an entrepreneur; and indeed, he is the last of the competitive entrepreneurs.

The degree of organization in hustling depends frequently on the kind of hustling. Regular pimping and pushing require many trusted contacts and organization. Regular stealing requires regular fences for hot goods. But in Ghost-town when the hustler moved, he usually moved alone and on a small scale. His success was on him. He could not depend on the support of some benevolent organization. Alone, without a sure way of running the same game twice, he must continually recalculate conditions and people and find new ways of taking or be taken himself. The phrase "free enterprise for the poor and socialism for the rich" applies only too well in the streets. The political conservative should applaud all that individual initiative.

Negro street time is built around the irrelevance of clock time, white man's time, and the relevance of street values and activities. Like anyone else, a street dude is on time by the standard clock whenever he wants to be, not on time when he does not want to be and does not have to be.

When the women in school hit the street at the lunch

hour and he wants to throw them a rap, he will be there then and not one hour after they have left. But he may be kicked out of high school for truancy or lose his job for being late and unreliable. He learned at an early age that school and job were neither interesting nor salient to his way of life. A regular on the set will readily admit being crippled by a lack of formal education. Yet school was a "bum kick." It was not his school. The teachers put him down for his dress, hair, and manners. As a human being he has feelings of pride and autonomy, the very things most threatened in those institutional situations where he was or is the underdeveloped, unrespected, illiterate, and undeserving outsider. Thus whatever "respectable" society says will help him, he knows oppresses him, and he retreats to the streets for security and a larger degree of personal freedom. Here his control reaches a maximum, and he has the kind of autonomy which many middle class males might envy.

In the street, watches have a special and specific meaning. Watches are for pawning and not for telling time. When they are worn, they are decorations and ornaments of status. The street clock is informal, personal, and relaxed. It is not standardized nor easily synchronized to other clocks. In fact, a street dude may have almost infinite toleration for individual time schedules. To be on time is often meaningless, to be late an unconsciously accepted way of life. "I'll catch you later," or simply "later," are the street phrases that mean business will be taken care of, but not necessarily now.

Large areas of street life run on late time. For example, parties are not cut off by some built-in alarm clock of appointments and schedules. At least for the unemployed, standard time neither precedes nor follows the gig. Consequently, the action can take its course. It can last as long as interest is sustained and die by exhaustion or by the intrusion of some more interesting event. A gig may endure all night and well into another day. One of the reasons for the party assuming such time dimensions is purely economic. There are not enough cars and enough money for individual dates, so everyone converges in one place and takes care of as much business as possible there, that is, doing whatever is important at the time—sex, presentation of self, hustling.

Events starting late and lasting indefinitely are clearly street and class phenomena, not some special trait of Afro-Americans. Middle class Negroes who must deal with the organization and coordination of activities in church and elsewhere will jokingly and critically refer to a lack of standard time sense when they say that Mr. Jones arrived "CPT" (colored people's time). They have a word for it, because being late is a problem for people caught between two worlds and confronted with the task of meshing standard and street time. In contrast, the street dudes had no self-consciousness about being late; with few exceptions they had not heard the expression CPT. (When I questioned members of a middle class Negro fraternity, a sample matched by age to the street set, only three of the 25 interviewed could not define CPT. Some argued vehemently that CPT was the problem to be overcome.)

Personal time as expressed in parties and other street activities is not simply deficient knowledge and use of standard time. It is a positive adaption to generations of living whenever and wherever possible outside of the sound and control of the white man's clock. The personal clock is an adaptation to the chance and accidental character of events on the street and to the very positive value placed on emotion and feeling. (For a discussion of CPT which is close to some of the ideas presented here, see Jules

Henry, "White People's Time, Colored People's Time," *Trans-action*, March/April 1965.)

Chance reinforces personal time. A dude must be ready on short notice to move "where the action is." His internal clock may not be running at all when he is hanging on the corner and waiting for something to do. It may suddenly speed up by chance: Someone cruises by in a car and brings a nice "stash" of "weed," a gig is organized and he looks forward to being well togged-out and throwing a rap to some "boss chick," or a lame appears and opens himself to a quick "con." Chance as a determinant of personal time can be called more accurately *uncertain predictability*. Street life is an aggregate of relatively independent events. A dude may not know exactly what or when something will happen, but from past experience he can predict a range of possibilities, and he will be ready, in position, and waiting.

In white middle class stereotypes and fears—and in reality—street action is highly expressive. A forthright yet stylized expression of emotion is positively evaluated and most useful. Street control and communication are based on personal power and the direct impingement of one individual on another. Where there is little property, status in the set is determined by personal qualities of mind and brawn.

The importance of emotion and expression appears again and again in street tongue and ideology. When asked, "How does a dude make a rep on the set?" over half of the sample mentioned "style," and all could discuss the concept. Style is difficult to define as it has so many referents. It means to carry one's self well, dress well, to show class. In the ideology of the street, it may be a way of behaving. One has style if he is able to dig people as they are. He doesn't put them down for what they do. He shows toleration. But a person with style must also show respect. That means respect for a person as he is, and since there is power in the street, respect for another's superior power. Yet one must show respect in such a way that he is able to look tough and inviolate, fearless, secure, "cool."

Style may also refer to the use of gestures in conversation or in dance. It may be expressed in the loose walk, the jivey or dancing walk, the slow cool walk, the way one "chops" or "makes it" down the street. It may be the loose, relaxed hand rap or hand slap, the swinger's greeting which is used also in the hip middle class teen sets. There are many refined variations of the hand rap. As a greeting, one may simply extend his hand, palm up. Another slaps it loosely with his finger. Or, one person may be standing with his hand behind and palm up. Another taps the hand in passing, and also pays his respect verbally with the conventional greeting "What's happening, Brother." Or, in conversation, the hand may be slapped when an individual has "scored," has been "digging," has made a point, has got through to the person.

Style is a comparatively neutral value compared to "soul." Soul can be many things—a type of food (good food is "soul food," a "bowl of soul"), music, a quality of mind, a total way of acting (in eating, drinking, dancing, walking, talking, relating to others, etc.). The person who acts with soul acts directly and honestly from his heart. He feels it and tells it "like it is." One respondent identified soul with ambition and drive. He said the person with soul, once he makes up his mind, goes directly to the goal, doesn't change his mind, doesn't wait and worry about messing up a little. Another said soul was getting down to the nitty-gritty, that is, moving directly to what is basic without guise and disguise. Thus soul is the opposite of hypocrisy, deceit, and phoniness, the opposite of "affective neutrality," and "instrumentality." Soul is simply whatever is considered beautiful, honest, and virtuous in men.

Most definitions tied soul directly to Negro experience. As one hustler put it, "It is the ability to survive. We've made it with so much less. Soul is the Negro who has the spirit to sing in slavery to overcome the monotony." With very few exceptions, the men interviewed argued that soul was what Negroes had and whites did not. Negroes were "soul brothers," warm and emotional—whites cold as ice. Like other oppressed minorities these street Negroes believed they had nothing except their soul and their humanity, and that this made them better than their oppressors.

Soul is anchored in a past and present of exploitation and deprivation, but are there any street values and activities which relate to the future? The regular in the street set has no providential mission; he lives personally and instrumentally in the present, yet he dreams about the day when he will get himself together and move ahead to the rewards of a good job, money, and a family. Moreover, the personal dream coexists with a nascent political nationalism, the belief that Negroes can and will make it as Negroes. His present-future time is a combination of contradictions and developing possibilities. Here I will be content to document without weighing two aspects of his orientation: *fantasy personal future* and *fantasy collective future*. I use the word fantasy because street people have not yet the knowledge and means and perhaps the will to fulfill their dreams. It is hard enough to survive by the day.

When the members of the set were asked, "What do you really want out of life?" their responses were conventional, concrete, seemingly realistic, and—given their skills—rather hopeless. Two-thirds of the sample mentioned material aspirations—the finer things in life, a home, security, a family. For example, one said, in honest street language, "I want to get things for my kids and to make sure they have a father." Another said, jokingly, "a good future, a home, two or three girls living with me." Only one person didn't know, and the others deviated a little from the material response. They said such things as "for everyone to be on friendly terms—a better world . . . then I could get all I wish," "to be free," "to help people."

But if most of the set wanted money and security, they wanted it on their own terms. As one put it, "I don't want to be in a middle class bag, but I would like a nice car, home, and food in the icebox." He wanted the things and the comforts of middle class life, but not the hypocrisy, the venality, the coldness, the being forced to do what one does not want to do. All that was in the middle class bag. Thus the home and the money may be ends in themselves, but also fronts, security for carrying on the usual street values. Street people believed that they already had something that was valuable and looked down upon the person who made it and moved away into the middle class world. For the observer, the myths are difficult to separate from the truths—here where the truths are so bitter. One can only say safely that street people dream of a high status, and they really do not know how to get it.

The Negro dudes are political outsiders by the usual poll questions. They do not vote. They do not seek out civil rights demonstrations. They have very rudimentary knowledge of political organization. However, about the age of 18, when fighting and being tough are less important than before, street people begin to discuss their position in society. Verbally they care very much about the politics of race and the future of the Negro. The topic is always a ready catalyst for a soul session.

The political consciousness of the street can be summarized by noting those interview questions which attracted at least a 75 percent rate of agreement. The typical respondent was angry. He approves of the Watts incident, although from his isolated corner of the city he did not actively participate. He knows something about the history of discrimination and believes that if something isn't done soon America can expect violence: "What this country needs is a revolutionary change." He is more likely to praise the leadership of Malcolm X than Lyndon Johnson, and he is definitely opposed to the Vietnam war. The reason for his opposition is clear: Why fight for a country which is not mine, when the fight is here?

Thus his racial consciousness looks to the future and a world where he will not have to stand in the shadow of the white man. But his consciousness has neither clear plan nor political commitment. He has listened to the Muslims, and he is not a black nationalist. True, the Negro generally has more soul than the white. He thinks differently, his women may be different, yet integration is preferable to separatism. Or, more accurately, he doesn't quite understand what all these terms mean. His nationalism is real as a folk nationalism based on experience with other Negroes and isolation from whites.

The significance of a racial future in the day to day consciousness of street people cannot be assessed. It is a developing possibility dependent on unforeseen conditions beyond the scope of their skill and imagination. But bring up the topic of race and tomorrow, and the dreams come rushing in—dreams of superiority, dreams of destruction, dreams of human equality. These dreams of the future are salient. They are not the imagination of authoritarian personalities, except from the viewpoint of those who see spite lurking behind every demand for social change. They are certainly not the fantasies of the hipster living philosophically in the present without hope and ambition. One hustler summarized the Negro street concept of ambition and future time when he said:

> The Negro has more ambition than the whites. He's got farther to go. "The man" is already there. But we're on your trail, daddy. You still have smoke in our eyes, but we're catching up.

April 1967

FURTHER READING SUGGESTED BY THE AUTHOR:

Manchild in the Promised Land by Claude Brown (New York: The New American Library, 1966). An autobiographical account of street life in Harlem.

Street Corner Society by William Foote Whyte (Chicago: University of Chicago Press, 1943). A sociological account of street life among Italian-Americans in Boston.

The Voices of Time edited by J. T. Fraser (New York: George Braziller, 1965). Essays on man's views of time as expressed by the sciences and the humanities.

The Silent Language by Edward T. Hall (Greenwich, Conn.: Fawcett Publications, 1963). An anthropologist describes how time and other cultural concepts are communicated without the use of words.

Rapping in the Ghetto

THOMAS KOCHMAN

"Rapping," "shucking," "jiving," "running it down," "gripping," "copping a plea," "signifying" and "sounding" are all part of the black ghetto idiom and describe different kinds of talking. Each has its own distinguishing features of form, style, and function; each is influenced by, and influences, the speaker, setting, and audience; and each sheds light on the black perspective and the black condition—on those orienting values and attitudes that will cause a speaker to speak or perform in his own way within the social context of the black community.

I was first introduced to black idiom in New York City, and, as a professional linguist interested in dialects, I began to compile a lexicon of such expressions. My real involvement, however, came in Chicago, while preparing a course on black idiom at the Center for Inner City studies, the southside branch of Northeastern Illinois State College.

Here I began to explore the full cultural significance of

this kind of verbal behavior. My students and informants within black Chicago, through their knowledge of
these terms, and their ability to recognize and categorize
the techniques, and to give examples, gave me much re-
liable data. When I turned for other or better examples to the literature—such as the writings of Malcolm X,
Robert Conot, and Iceberg Slim—my students and informants were able to recognize and confirm their authenticity.

While often used to mean ordinary conversation, rapping
is distinctively a fluent and a lively way of talking, always
characterized by a high degree of personal style. To one's
own group, rapping may be descriptive of an interesting
narration, a colorful rundown of some past event. An
example of this kind of rap is the answer from a Chicago
gang member to a youth worker who asked how his
group became organized:

Now I'm goin tell you how the jive really started.
I'm goin to tell you how the club got this big. 'Bout 1956
there used to be a time when the Jackson Park show was
open and the Stony show was open. Sixty-six street,
Jeff, Gene, all of 'em, little bitty dudes, little bitty . . .
Gene wasn't with 'em then. Gene was cribbin (living)
over here. Jeff, all of 'em, real little bitty dudes, you dig?
All of us were little.

Sixty-six (the gang on sixty-sixth street), they
wouldn't allow us in the Jackson Park show. That was
when the parky (?) was headin it. Everybody say, If we
want to go to the show, we go! One day, who was it?
Carl Robinson. He went up to the show . . . and Jeff
fired on him. He came back and all this was swelled up
'bout yay big, you know. He come back over to the
hood (neighborhood). He told (name unclear) and
them dudes went up there. That was when mostly all
the main sixty-six boys was over here like Bett Riley.
All of 'em was over here. People that quit gang-bangin
(fighting, especially as a group), Marvell Gates, people

like that.

They went on up there, John, Roy and Skeeter went in there. And they start humbuggin (fighting) in there. That's how it all started. Sixty-six found out they couldn't beat us, at *that* time. They couldn't *whup* seven-o. Am I right Leroy? You was cribbin over here then. Am I right? We were dynamite! Used to be a time, you ain't have a passport, Man, you couldn't walk through here. And if didn't nobody know you it was worse than that. . . ."

Rapping to a woman is a colorful way of "asking for some pussy." "One needs to throw a lively rap when he is 'putting the make' on a broad." (John Horton, "Time and Cool People," *Trans*-action, April, 1967.)

According to one informant the woman is usually someone he has just seen or met, looks good, and might be willing to have sexual intercourse with him. My informant says the term would not be descriptive of talk between a couple "who have had a relationship over any length of time." Rapping then, is used at the beginning of a relationship to create a favorable impression and be persuasive at the same time. The man who has the reputation for excelling at this is the pimp, or mack man. Both terms describe a person of considerable status in the street hierarchy, who, by his lively and persuasive rapping ("macking" is also used in this context) has acquired a stable of girls to hustle for him and give him money. For most street men and many teenagers he is the model whom they try to emulate. Thus, within the community you have a pimp walk, pimp style boots and clothes, and perhaps most of all "pimp talk," is a colorful literary example of a telephone rap. One of my informants regards it as extreme, but agrees that it illustrates the language, style and technique of rapping. "Blood" is rapping to an ex-whore named Christine in an effort to trap her into his stable:

Now try to control yourself baby. I'm the tall stud

with the dreamy bedroom eyes across the hall in four-twenty. I'm the guy with the pretty towel wrapped around his sexy hips. I got the same hips on now that you X-rayed. Remember that hump of sugar your peepers feasted on?

She said, "Maybe, but you shouldn't call me. I don't want an incident. What do you want? A lady doesn't accept phone calls from strangers."

I said, "A million dollars and a trip to the moon with a bored, trapped, beautiful bitch, you dig? I'm no stranger. I've been popping the elastic on your panties ever since you saw me in the hall. . . ."

Rapping between men and women often is competitive and leads to a lively repartee with the women becoming as adept as the men. An example follows:

A man coming from the bathroom forgot to zip his pants. An unescorted party of women kept watching him and laughing among themselves. The man's friends "hip" (inform) him to what's going on. He approaches one woman—"Hey baby, did you see that big black Cadillac with the full tires? ready to roll in action just for you." She answers—"No mother-fucker, but I saw a little gray Volkswagen with two flat tires." Everybody laughs. His rap was "capped" (Excelled, topped).

When "whupping the game" on a "trick" or "lame" (trying to get goods or services from someone who looks like he can be swindled), rapping is often descriptive of the highly stylized verbal part of the maneuver. In well established "con games" the rap is carefully prepared and used with great skill in directing the course of the transaction. An excellent illustration came from an adept hustler who was playing the "murphy" game on a white trick. The "murphy" game is designed to get the *trick* to give his money to the hustler, who in this instance poses as a "steerer" (one who directs or steers customers to a brothel), to keep the whore from stealing it. The hustler then skips with the money.

Look Buddy, I know a fabulous house not more than two blocks away. Brother you ain't never seen more beautiful, freakier broads than are in that house. One of them, the prettiest one, can do more with a swipe than a monkey can with a banana. She's like a rubber doll; she can take a hundred positions."

At this point the sucker is wild to get to this place of pure joy. He entreats the con player to take him there, not just direct him to it.

The "murphy" player will prat him (pretend rejection) to enhance his desire. He will say, "Man, don't be offended, but Aunt Kate, that runs the house don't have nothing but highclass white men coming to her place. . . . You know, doctors, lawyers, big-shot politicians. You look like a clean-cut white man, but you ain't in that league are you? (Iceberg Slim, *Pimp: The Story of My Life*)

After a few more exchanges of the "murphy" dialogue, "the mark is separated from his scratch."

An analysis of rapping indicates a number of things.

■ For instance, it is revealing that one raps *to* rather than *with* a person supporting the impression that rapping is to be regarded more as a performance than verbal exchange. As with other performances, rapping projects the personality, physical appearance and style of the performer. In each of the examples given, the intrusive "I" of the speaker was instrumental in contributing to the total impression of the rap.

■ The combination of personality and style is usually best when "asking for some pussy." It is less when "whupping the game" on someone or "running something down."

In "asking for some pussy" for example, where personality and style might be projected through non-verbal means: stance, clothing, walking, looking, one can speak of a "silent rap." The woman is won here without the use of words, or rather, with words being implied that would generally accompany the non-verbal components.

■ As a lively way of "running it down" the verbal element consists of personality and style plus information. To someone *reading* my example of the gang member's narration, the impression might be that the information would be more influential in directing the listener's response. The youth worker might be expected to say "So that's how the gang got so big," instead of "Man, that gang member is *bad* (strong, brave)" in which instance he would be responding to the personality and style of the rapper. However, if the reader would *listen* to the gang member on tape or could have been present when the gang member spoke he more likely would have reacted more to personality and style as my informants did.

Remember that in attendance with the youth worker were members of the gang who *already knew* how the gang got started (e.g. "Am I right Leroy? You was cribbin' over here then") and for whom the information itself would have little interest. Their attention was held by the *way* the information was presented.

■ The verbal element in "whupping the game" on someone, in the preceding example, was an integral part of an overall deception in which information and personality-style were skillfully manipulated for the purpose of controlling the "trick's" response. But again, greater weight must be given to personality-style. In the "murphy game" for example, it was this element which got the trick to trust the hustler and leave his money with him for "safe-keeping."

The function of rapping in each of these forms is *expressive*. By this I mean that the speaker raps to project his personality onto the scene or to evoke a generally favorable response. When rapping is used to "ask for some pussy" or to "whup the game" on someone its function is *directive*. By this I mean that rapping becomes an instrument to manipulate and control people to get them to give up or to do something. The difference between rapping to a "fox" (pretty girl) for the purpose of "getting inside her pants" and rapping to a "lame" to get something from him is operational rather than functional. The latter rap contains a concealed motivation where the former does not.

"Shucking," "shucking it," "shucking and jiving," "S-ing" and "J-ing" or just "jiving," are terms that refer to language behavior practiced by the black when confronting "the Man" (the white man, the establishment, or *any* authority figure), and to another form of language behavior practiced by blacks with each other on the peer group level.

In the South, and later in the North, the black man learned that American society had assigned to him a restrictive role and status. Among whites his behavior had to conform to this imposed station and he was constantly reminded to "keep his place." He learned that it was not acceptable in the presence of white people to show feelings of indignation, frustration, discontent, pride, ambition, or desire; that real feelings had to be concealed behind a mask of innocence, ignorance, childishness, obedience, humility and deference. The terms used by the black to describe the role he played before white folks in the South was "tomming" or "jeffing." Failure to accommodate the white Southerner in this respect was almost certain to invite psychological and often physical brutality. A description related by a black psychiatrist, Alvin F. Poussaint, is typical and revealing:

Once last year as I was leaving my office in Jackson, Miss., with my Negro secretary, a white policeman yelled, "Hey, boy! Come here!" Somewhat bothered, I retorted: "I'm no boy!" He then rushed at me, inflamed, and stood towering over me, snorting "What d'ja say, boy?" Quickly he frisked me and demanded, "What's your name boy?" Frightened, I replied, "Dr. Poussaint. I'm a physician." He angrily chuckled and hissed, "What's your first name, boy?" When I hesitated he assumed a threatening stance and clenched his fists. As my heart palpitated, I muttered in profound humiliation,

"Alvin."

He continued his psychological brutality, bellowing, "Alvin, the next time I call you, you come right away, you hear? You hear?" I hesitated. "You hear me, boy?" My voice trembling with helplessness, but *following my instincts of self-preservation,* I murmured, "Yes, sir." *Now fully satisfied that I had performed and acquiesced to my "boy" status,* he dismissed me with, "Now, boy, go on and get out of here or next time we'll take you for a little ride down to the station house! (Alvin F. Poussaint, "A Negro Psychiatrist Explains the Negro Psyche," *The New York Times Magazine,* August 20, 1967), (emphasis mine).

In the northern cities the black encountered authority figures equivalent to Southern "crackers": policemen, judges, probation officers, truant officers, teachers and "Mr. Charlies" (bosses), and soon learned that the way to get by and avoid difficulty was to shuck. Thus, he learned to accommodate "the Man," to use the total orchestration of speech, intonation, gesture and facial expression for the purpose of producing whatever appearance would be acceptable. It was a technique and ability that was developed from fear, a respect for power, and a will to survive. This type of accommodation is exemplified by the Uncle Tom with his "Yes sir, Mr. Charlie," or "Anything you say, Mr. Charlie."

Through accommodation, many blacks became adept at concealing and controlling their emotions and at assuming a variety of postures. They became competent actors. Many developed a keen perception of what affected, motivated, appeased or satisfied the authority figures with whom they came into contact. Shucking became an effective way for many blacks to stay out of trouble, and for others a useful artifice for avoiding arrest or getting out of trouble when apprehended. Shucking it with a judge, for example, would be to feign repentance in the hope of receiving a lighter or suspended sentence. Robert Conot reports an example of shucking in his book, *Rivers of Blood, Years of Darkness:* Joe was found guilty of possession of narcotics. But he did an excellent job of shucking it with the probation officer.

The probation officer interceded for Joe with the judge: "His own attitude toward the present offense appears to be serious and responsible and it is believed that the defendant is an excellent subject for probation."

Some field illustrations of shucking to get out of trouble came from some seventh grade children from an inner-city school in Chicago. The children were asked to talk their way out of a troublesome situation.

■ You are cursing at this old man and your mother comes walking down the stairs. She hears you.

To "talk your way out of this":

"I'd tell her that I was studying a scene in school for a play."

■ What if you were in a store stealing something and the manager caught you?

"I would start stuttering. Then I would say, 'Oh, Oh, I forgot. Here the money is.'"

A literary example of shucking comes from Iceberg Slim's autobiography. Iceberg, a pimp, shucks before "two red-faced Swede rollers (detectives)" who catch him in a motel room with his whore. My italics identify which elements of the passage constitute the shuck.

I put my shaking hands into the pajama pockets . . . *I hoped I was keeping the fear out of my face. I gave them a wide toothy smile.* They came in and stood in the middle of the room. Their eyes were racing about the room. Stacy was open mouthed in the bed.

I said, *"Yes gentlemen, what can I do for you?"*

Lanky said, "We wanta see your I.D."

I went to the closet and got the phony John Cato Fredrickson I.D. I put it in his palm. I felt cold sweat running down my back. They looked at it, then looked at each other.

Lanky said, "You are in violation of the law. You signed the motel register improperly. Why didn't you sign your full name? What are you trying to hide? What are you doing here in town? It says here you're a dancer. We don't have a club in town that books entertainers."

I said, *"Officers, my professional name is Johnny Cato. I've got nothing to hide. My full name had always been too long for the marquees. I've fallen into the habit of using the shorter version.*

"My legs went out last year. I don't dance anymore. My wife and I decided to go into business. We are making a tour of this part of the country. We think that in your town we've found the ideal site for a Southern fried chicken shack. My wife has a secret recipe that should make us rich up here." (Iceberg Slim, *Pimp: The Story of My Life*)

Another example of shucking was related to me by a colleague. A black gang member was coming down the stairway from the club room with seven guns on him and encountered some policemen and detectives coming up the same stairs. If they stopped and frisked him he and others would have been arrested. A paraphrase of his shuck follows: "Man, I gotta get away from up there. There's gonna be some trouble and I don't want no part of it." This shuck worked on the minds of the policemen. It anticipated their questions as to why he was leaving the club room, and why he would be in a hurry. He also gave *them* a reason for wanting to get up to the room fast.

It ought to be mentioned at this point that there was not uniform agreement among my informants in characterizing the above examples as shucking. One informant used shucking only in the sense in which it is used among peers, e.g., bull-shitting, and characterized the above examples as jiving or whupping game. Others however, identified the above examples as shucking, and reserved jiving and whupping game for more offensive maneuvers. In fact, one of the apparent features of shucking is that the posture of the black when acting with members of the establishment be a *defensive* one.

Frederick Douglass, in telling of how he taught himself to read, would challenge a white boy with whom he was playing, by saying that he could write as well as he. Whereupon he would write down all the letters he knew. The white boy would then write down more letters than Douglass did. In this way, Douglass eventually learned all the letters of the alphabet. Some of my informants regarded the example as whupping game. Others regarded it as shucking. The former were perhaps focusing on the manuever rather than the language used. The latter may have felt that any maneuvers designed to learn to read were justifiably defensive. One of my informants said Douglass was "shucking *in order to* whup the game." This latter response seems to be the most revealing. Just as one can rap to whup the game on someone, so one can shuck or jive for the same purpose; that is, assume a guise or posture or perform some action in a certain way that is designed to work on someone's mind to get him to give up something.

The following examples from Malcolm X illustrate the shucking and jiving in this context though jive is the term used. Today, whupping game might also be the term used to describe the operation. Whites who came at night got a better reception; the several Harlem nightclubs they patronized were geared to entertain and jive (flatter, cajole) the night white crowd to get their money. (Malcolm X, *The Autobiography of Malcolm X*)

The maneuvers involved here are clearly designed to obtain some benefit or advantage.

Freddie got on the stand and went to work on his own shoes. Brush, liquid polish, brush, paste wax, shine rag, lacquer sole dressing . . . step by step, Freddie showed me what to do.

"But you got to get a whole lot faster. You can't waste time!" Freddie showed me how fast on my own shoes. Then because business was tapering off, he had time to give me a demonstration of how to make the shine rag pop like a firecracker. "Dig the action?" he asked. He did it in slow motion. I got down and tried it on his shoes. I had the principle of it. "Just got to do it, faster," Freddie said. *"It's a jive noise, that's all. Cats tip better, they figure you're knocking yourself out!"* (Malcolm X, *The Autobiography of Malcolm X*)

An eight year old boy whupped the game on me one day this way:

My colleague and I were sitting in a room listening to a tape. The door to the room was open and outside was a soda machine. Two boys came up in the elevator, stopped at the soda machine, and then came into the room.

"Do you have a dime for two nickels?" Presumably the soda machine would not accept nickels. I took out the change in my pocket, found a dime and gave it to the boy for two nickels.

After accepting the dime, he looked at the change in my hand and asked, "Can I have two cents? I need carfare to get home." I gave him the two cents.

At first I assumed the verbal component of the maneuver was the rather weak, transparently false reason for wanting the two cents. Actually, as was pointed out to me later, the maneuver began with the first question which was designed to get me to show my money. He could then ask me for something that he knew I had, making my refusal more difficult. He apparently felt that the reason need not be more than plausible because the amount he wanted was small. Were the amount larger, he would no doubt have elaborated on the verbal element of the game. The form of the verbal element could be in the direction of rapping or shucking and jiving. If he were to rap the eight-year old might say, "Man, you know a cat needs to have a little bread to keep the girls in line." Were he to shuck and jive he might make the reason for needing the money more compelling, look hungry, etc.

The function of shucking and jiving as it refers to blacks and "the Man" is designed to work on the mind and emotions of the authority figure for the purpose of getting him to feel a certain way or give up something that will be to the other's advantage. Iceberg showed a "toothy smile" which said to the detective, "I'm glad to see you" and "Would I be glad to see you if I had something to hide?" When the maneuvers seem to be *defensive* most of my informants regarded the language behavior as shucking. When the maneuvers were *offensive* my informants tended to regard the behavior as 'whupping the game.'

Also significant is that the first form of shucking described, which developed out of accommodation, is becoming less frequently used today by many blacks, because of a new found self-assertiveness and pride, challenging the system. The willingness on the part of many blacks to accept the psychological and physical brutality and general social consequences of not "keeping one's place" is indicative of the changing self-concept of the black man. Ironically, the shocked reaction of some whites to the present militancy of the black is partly due to the fact that the black was so successful at "putting Whitey on" via shucking in the past. This new attitude can be seen from a conversation I recently had with a shoe shine attendant at O'Hare airport in Chicago.

I was having my shoes shined and the black attendant was using a polishing machine instead of the rag that was generally used in the past. I asked whether the machine made his work any easier. He did not answer me until about ten seconds had passed and then responded in a loud voice that he "never had a job that was easy," that he would give me "one hundred dollars for any *easy* job" I could offer him, that the machine made his job "faster" but not "easier." I was startled at the response because it was so unexpected and I realized that here was a new "breed of cat" who was not going to shuck for a big tip or ingratiate himself with "Whitey" anymore. A few years ago his response probably would have been different.

The contrast between this "shoe-shine" scene and the one illustrated earlier from Malcolm X's autobiography, when "shucking Whitey" was the common practice, is striking.

Shucking, jiving, shucking and jiving, or S-ing and J-ing, when referring to language behavior practiced by blacks, is descriptive of the talk and gestures that are appropriate to "putting someone on" by creating a false impression. The terms seem to cover a range from simply telling a lie, to bullshitting, to subtly playing with someone's mind. An important difference between this form of shucking and that described earlier is that the same talk and gestures that are deceptive to the "the Man" are often transparent to those members of one's own group who are able practitioners at shucking themselves. As Robert Conot has pointed out, "The Negro who often fools the white officer by 'shucking it' is much less likely to be successful with another Negro. . . ." Also, S-ing and J-ing within the group often has play overtones in which the person being "put on" is aware of the attempts being made and goes along with it for enjoyment or in appreciation of the style.

"Running it down" is the term used by speakers in the ghetto when it is their intention to give information, either by explanation, narrative, or giving advice. In the following literary example, Sweet Mac is "running this Edith broad down" to his friends:

Edith is the "saved" broad who can't marry out of her religion . . . or do anything else out of her religion for that matter, especially what I wanted her to do. A bogue religion, man! So dig, for the last couple weeks I been quoting the Good Book and all that stuff to her; telling her I am now saved myself, you dig.

(Woodie King, Jr., "The Game," *Liberator,* August, 1965)

The following citation from Claude Brown uses the term with the additional sense of giving advice:

If I saw him (Claude's brother) hanging out with cats I knew were weak, who might be using drugs sooner or later, I'd run it down to him.

It seems clear that running it down has simply an informative function, that of telling somebody something that he doesn't already know.

"Gripping" is of fairly recent vintage, used by black high school students in Chicago to refer to the talk and facial expression that accompanies a *partial* loss of face or self-possession, or showing of fear. Its appearance alongside "copping a plea," which refers to a total loss of face, in which one begs one's adversary for mercy, is a significant new perception. In linking it with the street code which acclaims the ability to "look tough and inviolate, fearless, secure, 'cool,' " it suggests that even the slightest weakening of this posture will be held up to ridicule and contempt. There are always contemptuous overtones attached to the use of the term when applied to the others' behavior. One is tempted to link it with the violence and toughness required to survive on the street. The intensity of both seems to be increasing. As one of my informants noted, "Today, you're *lucky* if you end up in the hospital"—that is, are not killed.

Both gripping and copping a plea refer to behavior produced from fear and a respect for superior power. An example of gripping comes from the record "*Street and Gangland Rhythms*" (Band 4 Dumb Boy). Lennie meets Calvin and asks him what happened to his lip. Calvin says that a boy named Pierre hit him for copying off him in school. Lennie, pretending to be Calvin's brother, goes to confront Pierre. Their dialogue follows:

Lennie: "Hey you! What you hit my little brother for?"
Pierre: "Did he tell you what happen man?"

Lennie: "Yeah, he told me what happened."

Pierre: "But you . . . but you . . . but you should tell your people to teach him to go to school, man." (Pause) I, I know, I know I didn't have a right to hit him."

Pierre, anticipating a fight with Lennie if he continued to justify his hitting of Calvin, tried to avoid it by "gripping" with the last line.

Copping a plea, originally meant "To plead guilty to a lesser charge to save the state the cost of a trial," (with the hope of receiving a lesser or suspended sentence) but is now generally used to mean 'to beg,' 'plead for mercy,' as in the example "Please cop, don't hit me. I give." (*Street and Gangland Rhythms,* Band 1 "Gang Fight"). This change of meaning can be seen from its used by Piri Thomas in *Down These Mean Streets.*

The night before my hearing, I decided to make a prayer. It had to be on my knees, 'cause if I was gonna cop a plea to God, I couldn't play it cheap.

The function of gripping and copping a plea is obviously to induce pity or to acknowledge the presence of superior strength. In so doing, one evinces noticeable feelings of fear and insecurity which also result in a loss of status among one's peers.

Signifying is the term used to describe the language behavior that, as Abrahams has defined it, attempts to "imply, goad, beg, boast by indirect verbal or gestural means." (Roger D. Abrahams, *Deep Down in the Jungle*) In Chicago it is also used as a synonym to describe language behavior more generally known as "sounding" elsewhere.

Some excellent examples of signifying as well as of other forms of language behavior come from the well known "toast" (narrative form) "The Signifying Monkey and the Lion" which was collected by Abrahams from Negro street corner bards in Philadelphia. In the above toast the monkey is trying to get the lion involved in a fight with the elephant:

> Now the lion came through the jungle one peaceful
> day,
> When the signifying monkey stopped him, and that is
> what he started to say:
> He said, "Mr. Lion," he said, "A bad-assed mother-
> fucker down your way,"
> He said, "Yeah! The way he talks about your folks is
> a certain shame.
> "I even heard him curse when he mentioned your
> grandmother's name."
> The lion's tail shot back like a forty-four
> When he went down that jungle in all uproar.

Thus the monkey has goaded the lion into a fight with
the elephant by "signifying," that is, indicating that the
elephant has been "sounding on" (insulting) the lion.
When the lion comes back, thoroughly beaten up, the
monkey again "signifies" by making fun of the lion:

> . . . lion came back through the jungle more dead than
> alive,
> When the monkey started some more of that signifying
> jive.
> He said, "Damn, Mr. Lion, you went through here yes-
> terday, the jungle rung.
> Now you come back today, damn near hung."

The monkey, of course, is delivering this taunt from a
safe distance away on the limb of a tree when his foot
slips and he falls to the ground, at which point,

> Like a bolt of lightning, a stripe of white heat,
> The lion was on the monkey with all four feet.

In desperation the monkey quickly resorts to "copping a
plea":

> The monkey looked up with a tear in his eyes,
> He said, "Please, Mr. Lion, I apologize."

His "plea" however, fails to move the lion to show any
mercy so the monkey tries another verbal ruse, "shucking":

> He said, "You lemme get my head out of the sand,

ass out the grass, I'll fight you like a natural man."
In this he is more successful as,

The lion jumped back and squared for a fight.
The motherfucking monkey jumped clear out of sight.

A safe distance away again, the monkey returns to "signifying":

He said, "Yeah, you had me down, you had me at last,
But you left me free, now you can still kiss my ass."

This example illustrates the methods of provocation,
goading and taunting artfully practiced by a signifier.

Interestingly, when the *function* of signifying is *directive* the *tactic* employed is *indirection*, i.e., the signifier
reports or repeats what someone else has said about the
listener; the "report" is couched in plausible language designed to compel belief and arouse feelings of anger and
hostility. There is also the implication that if the listener
fails to do anything about it—what has to be "done"
is usually quite clear—his status will be seriously compro-
mised. Thus the lion is compelled to vindicate the honor
of his family by fighting or else leave the impression that
he is afraid, and that he is not "king" of the jungle.
When used for the purpose of directing action, "signifying" is like "shucking" in also being deceptive and subtle
in approach and depending for success on the naivete or
gullibility of the person being "put on."

When the function of signifying is to arouse feelings
of embarrassment, shame, frustration or futility, to diminish someone's status, the tactic employed is direct in
the form of a taunt, as in the example where the monkey
is making fun of the lion.

Sounding is the term which is today most widely known
for the game of verbal insult known in the past as "Playing
the Dozens," "The Dirty Dozens" or just "The Dozens."
Other current names for the game have regional distribution: Signifying or "Sigging" (Chicago), Joning (Washington, D.C.), Screaming (Harrisburg), etc. In Chicago,
the term "sounding" would be descriptive of the initial

remarks which are designed to sound out the other person to see whether he will play the game. The verbal insult is also subdivided, the term "signifying" applying to insults which are hurled directly at the person and the dozens applying to results hurled at your opponent's family, especially, the mother.

Sounding is often catalyzed by signifying remarks referred to earlier such as "Are you going to let him say that about your mama" to spur an exchange between members of the group. It is begun on a relatively low key and built up by verbal exchanges. The game goes like this:

One insults a member of another's family; others in the group make disapproving sounds to spur on the coming exchange. The one who has been insulted feels at this point that he must reply with a slur on the protagonist's family which is clever enough to defend his honor (And therefore that of his family). This, of course, leads the other (once again, more due to pressure from the crowd than actual insult) to make further jabs. This can proceed until everyone is bored with the whole affair, until one hits the other (fairly rare), or until some other subject comes up that interrupts the proceedings (the usual state of affairs). (Roger D. Abrahams, "Playing the Dozens," *Journal of American Folklore,* July-September, 1962)

Mack McCormick describes the dozens as a verbal contest:

in which the players strive to bury one another with vituperation. In the play, the opponent's mother is especially slandered . . . Then, in turn fathers are identified as queer and syphilitic. Sisters are whores, brothers are defective, cousins are "funny" and the opponent is himself diseased. (Mack McCormick, "The Dirty Dozens," book jacket in the record album *The Unexpurgated Folksongs of Men,* Arhoolie Records).

An example of the "game" collected by one of my

students goes:

Frank looked up and saw Leroy enter the Outpost. Leroy walked past the room where Quinton, "Nap," "Pretty Black," "Cunny," Richard, Haywood, "Bull" and Reese sat playing cards. As Leroy neared the T.V. room, Frank shouted to him.

Frank: "Hey Leroy, your mama—calling you man."

Leroy turned and walked toward the room where the sound came from. He stood in the door and looked at Frank.

Leroy: "Look motherfuckers, I don't play that shit."

Frank (signifying): "Man, I told you cats 'bout that mama jive" (as if he were concerned about how Leroy felt)

Leroy: "That's all right Frank; you don't have to tell these funky motherfuckers nothing; I'll fuck me up somebody yet."

Frank's face lit up as if he were ready to burst his side laughing. "Cunny" became pissed at Leroy.

Cunny: "Leroy, you stupid bastard, you let Frank make a fool of you. He said that 'bout your mama."

"Pretty Black": "Aw, fat ass head 'Cunny' shut up."

"Cunny": Ain't that some shit. This black slick head motor flicker got nerve 'nough to call somebody 'fat-head.' Boy, you so black, you sweat Permalube Oil."

This eased the tension of the group as they burst into loud laughter.

"Pretty Black": "What 'chu laughing 'bout 'Nap,' with your funky mouth smelling like dog shit."

Even Leroy laughed at this.

"Nap": "Your mama motherfucker."

"Pretty Black": "Your funky mama too."

"Nap": (strongly) "It takes twelve barrels of water to make a steamboat run; it takes an elephant's dick to make your Grandmammy come; she been elephant fucked, camel fucked and hit side the head with your Grandpappy's nuts."

Reese: "Godorr-damn; go on and rap motherfucker." Reese began slapping each boy in his hand, giving his positive approval of "Naps" comment. "Pretty Black" in an effort not to be outdone, but directing his verbal play elsewhere stated:

"Pretty Black": "Reese, what you laughing 'bout? You so square, you shit bricked shit."

Frank: "Whoooowee!"

Reese (sounded back): "Square huh, what about your nappy ass hair before it was stewed; that shit was so bad till, when you went to bed at night, it would leave your head and go on the corner and meddle."

The boys slapped each other in the hand and cracked up.

"Pretty Black": "On the streets meddling, bet Dinky didn't offer me no pussy and I turned it down."

Frank: "Reese scared of pussy."

"Pretty Black": "Hell yeah; the greasy mother rather fuck old ugly, funky cock Sue Willie than get a piece of ass from a decent broad."

Frank: "Godorr-damn! Not Sue Willie."

"Pretty Black": "yeah ol meat-beating Reese rather screw that cross-eyed, clapsy bitch, who when she cry, tears rip down her ass."

Haywood: "Don't be so mean, Black"

Reese: "Aw shut up, you half-white bastard."

Frank: "Wait man, Haywood ain't gonna hear much more of that half-white shit; he's a brother too."

Reese: "Brother, my black ass; that white ass landlord gotta be this motherfucker's paw."

"Cunny": "Man, you better stop foolin with Haywood; he's turning red."

Haywood: "Fuck yall. (as he withdrew from the "sig" game.)

Frank: "Yeah, fuck yall; let's go to the stick hall."

The group left enroute to the billiard hall. (James Maryland, "Signifying at the Outpost," unpublished term paper for the course *Idiom of the Negro Ghettos,* January 1967)

The above example of sounding is an excellent illustration of the "game" as played by 15-17-year-old Negro boys, some of whom have already acquired the verbal skill which for them is often the basis for having a high "rep." Ability with words is apparently as highly valued as physical strength. In the sense that the status of one of the participants in the game is diminished if he has to resort to fighting to answer a verbal attack, verbal ability may be even more highly regarded than physical ability.

The relatively high value placed on verbal ability must be clear to most black boys at early age. Most boys begin their activity in sounding by compiling a repertoire of "one liners." When the game is played the one who has the greatest number of such remarks wins. Here are some examples of "one liners" collected from fifth and sixth grade black boys in Chicago:

Yo mama is so bowlegged, she looks like the bit out of a donut.

Yo mama sent her picture to the lonely hearts club, and they sent it back and said "We ain't that lonely!"

Your family is so poor the rats and roaches eat lunch out.

Your house is so small the roaches walk single file.

I walked in your house and your family was running around the table. I said, "Why you doin that?" Your mama say, "First one drops, we eat."

Real proficiency in the game comes to only a small percentage of those who play it. These players have the special skill in being able to turn around what their opponents have said and attack them with it. Thus, when someone indifferently said "fuck you" to Concho, his retort was immediate and devastating: "Man, you haven't even kissed me yet."

The "best talkers" from this group often become the successful street-corner, barber shop, and pool hall story tellers who deliver the long, rhymed, witty, narrative stories called "toasts." They are, as Roger D. Abrahams has described, the traditional "men of words" and have become on occasion entertainers such as Dick Gregory and Redd Fox, who are virtuosos at repartee, and preachers, whose verbal power has been traditionally esteemed.

The function of the "dozens" or "sounding" is to borrow status from an opponent through an exercise of verbal power. The opponent feels compelled to regain his status by "sounding" back on the speaker or other group member whom he regards as more vulnerable.

The presence of a group seems to be especially important in controlling the game. First of all, one does not "play" with just anyone since the subject matter is concerned with things that in reality one is quite sensitive about. It is precisely *because* "Pretty Black" has a "Black slick head" that makes him vulnerable to "Cunny's" barb, especially now when the Afro-American "natural" hair style is in vogue. Without the control of the group "sounding" will frequently lead to a fight. This was illustrated by a tragic epilogue concerning Haywood, when Haywood was being "sounded" on in the presence of two girls by his best friend (other members of the group were absent), he refused to tolerate it. He went home, got a rifle, came back and shot and killed his friend. In the classroom from about the fourth grade on fights among black boys invariably are caused by someone "sounding" on the other person's mother.

Significantly, the subject matter of sounding is changing with the changing self-concept of the black with regard to those physical characteristics that are characteristically "Negro," and which in the past were vulnerable points in the black psyche: blackness and "nappy" hair. It ought to be said that for many blacks, blackness was always highly esteemed and it might be more accurate to regard the present sentiment of the black community toward skin color as reflecting a shifted attitude for only a *portion* of the black community. This suggests that "sounding" on someone's light skin color is not new. Nevertheless, one can regard the previously favorable attitude toward light skin color and "good hair" as the prevailing one. "Other things being equal, the more closely a woman approached her white counterpart, the more attractive she was considered to be, by both men and women alike. "Good hair" (hair that is long and soft) and light skin were the chief criteria." (Elliot Liebow, *Tally's Corner*)

The dozens has been linked to the over-all psychosocial growth of the black male. McCormick has stated that a "single round of a dozen or so exchanges frees more pent-up aggressions than will a dose of sodium pentothal." The fact that one permits a kind of abuse within the rules of the game and within the confines of the group which would otherwise not be tolerated, is filled with psychological import. It seems also important, however, to view its function from the perspective of the non-participating members of the group. Its function for them may be to incite and prod individual members of the group to combat for the purpose of energizing the elements, of simply relieving the boredom of just "hanging around" and the malaise of living in a static and restrictive environment.

A summary analysis of the different forms of language behavior which have been discussed above permit the following generalizations:

The prestige norms which influence black speech behavior are those which have been successful in manipulating and controlling people and situations. The function of all of the forms of language behavior discussed above, with the exception of "running it down," was to project personality, assert oneself, or arouse emotion, frequently with the additional purpose of getting the person to give up or do something which will be of some benefit to the speaker. Only running it down has as its primary function to communicate information and often here too, the personality and style of the speaker in the form of rapping is projected along with the information.

The purpose for which language is used suggests that the speaker views the social situations into which he moves as consisting of a series of transactions which require that he be continually ready to take advantage of a person or situation or defend himself against being victimized. He has absorbed what Horton has called "street rationality." As one of Horton's respondents put it: "The good hustler . . . conditions his mind and must never put his guard too far down, to relax, or he'll be taken."

I have carefully avoided limiting the group within the black community of whom the language behavior and perspective of their environment is characteristic. While I have no doubt that it is true of those whom are generally called "street people" I am uncertain of the extent to which it is true of a much larger portion of the black community, especially the male segment. My informants consisted of street people, high school students, and blacks, who by their occupation as community and youth workers, possess what has been described as a "sharp sense of the streets." Yet it is difficult to find a black male in the community who has *not* witnessed or participated in the dozens or heard of signifying, or rapping, or shucking and jiving at some time during his growing up. It would be equally difficult to imagine a high school student in a Chicago inner city school not being touched by what is generally regarded as "street culture."

In conclusion, by blending style and verbal power, through rapping, sounding and running it down, the black in the ghetto establishes his personality; through shucking, gripping and copping a plea, he shows his respect for power; through jiving and signifying he stirs up excitement. With all of the above, he hopes to manipulate and control people and situations to give himself a winning edge.

February 1969

FURTHER READING SUGGESTED BY THE AUTHOR:
Deep Down in the Jungle by Roger D. Abrahams (Hatboro, Pa.: Folklore Associates, 1964) is a collection and analysis of black narrative folklore from the streets of Philadelphia.
Urban Blues by Charles Keil (Chicago: University of Chicago Press, 1966) is an analysis of the contemporary blues man as an "expressive male role within urban lower-class Negro culture."
Pimp, the Story of My Life by Iceberg Slim (Los Angeles: Holloway House, 1967) is a revealing insight into lower class life-styles.

The
Making of a Black Muslim

JOHN HOWARD

You were black enough to get in here. You had the courage
to stay. Now be man enough to follow the honorable Elijah
Muhammad. You have tried the devil's way. Now try the way
of the Messenger.

*Minister William X, in a West
Coast Black Muslim mosque*

The Lost-Found Nation of Islam in the Wilderness of
North America, commonly known as the Black Muslim
movement, claims a small but fanatically devoted membership among the Negroes of our major cities. The way
of the "Messenger" is rigorous for those who follow it.
The man or woman who becames a Muslim accepts not only
an ideology but an all-encompassing code that amounts
to a way of life.

A good Muslim does a full day's work on an empty
stomach. When he finally has his one meal of the day in
the evening, it can include no pork, nor can he have drink

before or a cigarette after; strict dietary rules are standard procedure, and liquor and smoking are forbidden under any circumstances. His recreation is likely to consist of reading the Koran or participating in a demanding round of temple-centered activities, running public meetings or aggressively proselytizing on the streets by selling the Muslim news-paper, *Muhammad Speaks*.

Despite allegations of Muslim violence (adverse pub-licity from the slaying of Malcolm X supports the erroneous notion that Muslims preach violence), the member's life is basically ascetic. Why then in a non-ascetic, hedonistical-ly-oriented society do people become Muslims? What is the life of a Muslim like? These are questions I asked in re-search among West Coast members. Specifically, I wanted to know:

■ What perspective on life makes membership in such an organization attractive?

■ Under what conditions does the potential recruit develop those perspectives?

■ How does he happen to come to the door of the temple for his first meeting?

■ The Black Muslims are a deviant organization even with-in the Negro community; the parents or friends of many members strongly objected to their joining. So how does the recruit handle pressures that might erode his allegiance to the organization and its beliefs?

Presenting my questions as an effort to "learn the truth" about the organization, I was able to conduct depth inter-views with 19 West Coast recruits, following them through the process of their commitment to the Nation of Islam.

Two main points of appeal emerged—black nationalism and an emphasis on self-help. Some recruits were attracted primarily by the first, and some by the second. The 14 inter-viewees who joined the organization for its aggressive black nationalism will be called "Muslim militants." The remaining five, who were attracted more by its emphasis on hard work and rigid personal morality, may be aptly termed "Protestant Ethic Muslims."

Of the 14 Muslim militants, some came from the South, some from border states, and some from the North. All lived in California at the time of the interviews; some migrated to the state as adults, others were brought out by their families as children. They varied in age from 24 to 46, and in education from a few years of grade school to four years of college. Regardless of these substantial differences in background, there were certain broad similarities among them.

At some point, each one had experiences that led away from the institutionally-bound ties and commitments that lend stability to most people's lives. Nine had been engaged in semi-legal or criminal activities. Two had been in the military, not as a career but as a way of postponing the decision of what to do for a living. None had a stable marital history. All of them were acutely aware of being outsiders by the standards of the larger society—and all had come to focus on race bias as the factor which denied them more conventional alternatives.

Leroy X came to California in his late teens, just before World War II:

I grew up in Kansas City, Missouri, and Missouri was a segregated state. Negroes in Kansas City were always restricted to the menial jobs. I came out here in 1940 and tried to get a job as a waiter. I was a trained waiter, but they weren't hiring any Negroes as waiters in any of the downtown hotels or restaurants. The best I could do was busboy, and they fired me from that when they found out I wasn't Filipino.

Leroy X was drafted, and after a short but stormy career

was given a discharge as being psychologically unfit.

I tried to get a job, but I couldn't so I started stealing. There was nothing else to do—I couldn't live on air. The peckerwoods didn't seem to give a damn whether I lived or died. They wouldn't hire me and didn't seem to worry how I was going to stay alive. I started stealing.

I could get you anything you wanted—a car, drugs, women, jewelry. Crime is a business like any other. I started off stealing myself. I wound up filling orders and getting rid of stuff. I did that for fifteen years. In between I did a little time. I did time for things I never thought of doing and went free for things I really did.

In my business you had no friends, only associates, and not very close ones at that. . . . I had plenty of money. I could get anything I wanted without working for it. It wasn't enough, though.

Bernard X grew up in New York City:

As a kid . . . you always have dreams—fantasies—of yourself doing something later—being a big name singer or something that makes you outstanding. But you never draw the connection between where you are and how you're going to get there. I had to—I can't say exactly when, 13, 14, 15, 16. I saw I was nowhere and had no way of getting anywhere.

Race feeling is always with you. You always know about The Man but I don't think it is real, really real, until you have to deal with it in terms of what you are going to do with your own life. That's when you feel it. If you just disliked him before—you begin to hate him when you see him blocking you in your life. I think then a sense of inevitability hits you and you see you're not going to make it out—up—away—anywhere—and you see The Man's part in the whole thing, that's when you begin to think thoughts about him.

Frederick 2X became involved fairly early in a criminal subculture. His father obtained a "poor man's divorce" by deserting the family. His mother had children by other men. Only a tenuous sense of belonging to a family existed. He was picked up by the police for various offenses several times before reaching his teens. The police patrolling his neighborhood eventually restricted him to a two-block area. There was, of course, no legal basis for this, but he was manhandled if seen outside that area by any policeman who knew him. He graduated in his late teens from "pot" to "shooting shit" and eventually spent time in Lexington.

William 2X, formerly a shoeshine boy, related the development of his perspective this way:

You know how they always talk about us running after white women. There have always been a lot of [white] servicemen in this town—half of them would get around to asking me to get a woman for them. Some of them right out, some of them backing into it, laughing and joking and letting me know how much they were my friend, building up to asking me where they could find some woman. After a while I began to get them for them. I ran women—both black and white. . . . What I hated was they wanted me to do something for them [find women] and hated me for doing it. They figure "any nigger must know where to find it. . . ."

Amos X grew up in an all-Negro town in Oklahoma and attended a Negro college. Because of this, he had almost no contact with whites during his formative years.

One of my aunts lived in Tulsa. I went to see her once when I was in college. I walked up to the front door of the house where she worked. She really got excited and told me if I came to see her anymore to come around to the back. But that didn't mean much to me at the time. It is only in looking back on it that all these things begin to add up.

After graduating from college, Amos joined the Marines.
There he began to "see how they [the whites] really felt"
about him; by the end of his tour, he had concluded that
"the white man is the greatest liar, the greatest cheat, the
greatest hypocrite on earth." Alienated and disillusioned,
he turned to professional gambling. Then, in an attempt at
a more conventional way of life, he married and took a
job teaching school.

> I taught English. Now I'm no expert in the slave masters'
> language, but I knew the way those kids talked after be-
> ing in school eight and nine years was ridiculous. They
> said things like "mens" for "men." I drilled them and
> pretty soon some of them at least in class began to sound
> like they had been inside a school. Now the principal
> taught a senior class in English and his kids talked as bad
> as mine. When I began to straighten out his kids also he
> felt I was criticizing him. . . . That little black man was
> afraid of the [white] superintendent and all those teach-
> ers were afraid. They had a little more than other so-
> called Negroes and didn't give a damn about those black
> children they were teaching. Those were the wages of
> honesty. It's one thing to want to do an honest job and
> another thing to be able to. . . .

With the collapse of his career as a public school teacher
and the break-up of his marriage, Amos went to California,
where he was introduced to the Muslim movement.

> I first heard about them [the Muslims] in 1961. There
> was a debate here between a Muslim and a Christian
> minister. The Muslims said all the things about Christian-
> ity which I had been thinking but which I had never
> heard anyone say before. He tore the minister up.

Finding an organization that aggressively rejected the
white man and the white man's religion, Amos found his

own point of view crystallized. He joined without hesitation.

Norman Maghid first heard of the Muslims while he was in prison.

I ran into one of the Brothers selling the paper about two weeks after I got out and asked him about the meetings. Whether a guy could just go and walk in. He told me about the meetings so I made it around on a Wednesday evening. I wasn't even bugged when they searched me. When they asked me about taking out my letter [joining the organization] I took one out. They seemed to know what they were talking about. I never believed in non-violence and love my enemies, especially when my enemies don't love me.

Muhammad Soule Kabah, born into a family of debt-ridden Texas sharecroppers, was recruited into the Nation of Islam after moving to California.

I read a series of articles in the Los Angeles *Herald Dispatch,* an exchange between Minister Henry and a Christian minister. It confirmed what my grandfather had told me about my African heritage, that I had nothing to be ashamed of, that there were six thousand books on mathematics in the Library of the University of Timbucktoo while Europeans were still wearing skins. Also my father had taught me never to kow-tow to whites. My own father had fallen away. My parents didn't want me to join the Nation. They said they taught hate. That's funny isn't it? The white man can blow up a church and kill four children and the black man worries that an organization which tells you not to just take it is teaching hate.

The Protestant Ethic Muslims all came from backgrounds with a strong tradition of Negro self-help. In two cases, the recruit's parents had been followers of Marcus Garvey;

another recruit explicitly endorsed the beliefs of Booker T. Washington; and the remaining two, coming from upwardly mobile families, were firm in the belief that Negroes could achieve higher status if they were willing to work for it.

When asked what had appealed to him about the Muslims, Norman X replied:

They thought that black people should do something for themselves. I was running this small place [a photography shop] and trying to get by. I've stuck with this place even when it was paying me barely enough to eat. Things always improve and I don't have to go to the white man for anything.

Ernestine X stressed similar reasons for joining the Muslims.

You learned to stand up straight and do something for yourself. You learn to be a lady at all times—to keep your house clean—to teach your children good manners. There is not a girl in the M-G-T who does not know how to cook and sew. The children are very respectful; they speak only when they are spoken to. There is no such thing as letting your children talk back to you the way some people believe. The one thing they feel is the Negroes' downfall is men and sex for the women, and women and sex for the men, and they frown on sex completely unless you are married.

Despite their middle-class attitudes in many areas, Protestant Ethic Muslims denounced moderate, traditional civil rights organizations such as the NAACP, just as vigorously as the militant Muslims did. Norman X said that he had once belonged to the NAACP but had dropped out.

They spent most of their time planning the annual brotherhood dinner. Besides it was mostly whites—whites and the colored doctors and lawyers who wanted to be white. As far as most Negroes were concerned they might as well not have existed.

Lindsey X, who had owned and run his own upholstery shop for more than 30 years, viewed the conventional black bourgeoisie with equal resentment.

I never belonged to the NAACP. What they wanted never seemed real to me. I think Negroes should create jobs for themselves rather than going begging for them. That's why I never supported CORE.

In this respect Norman and Lindsey were in full accord with the more militant Amos X, who asserted:

They [the NAACP and CORE] help just one class of people. . . . Let something happen to a doctor and they are right there; but if something happens to Old Mose on the corner, you can't find them.

The interviews made it clear that most of the Protestant Ethic Muslims had joined the Nation because, at some point, they began to feel the need of organizational support for their personal systems of value. For Norman and Lindsey, it was an attempt to stop what they considered their own backsliding after coming to California. Both mentioned drinking to excess and indulging in what they regarded as a profligate way of life. Guilt feelings apparently led them to seek Muslim support in returning to more enterprising habits.

The Nation of Islam is a deviant organization. As such it is subject to public scorn and ridicule. Thus it faces the problem of consolidating the recruit's allegiance in an environment where substantial pressures operate to erode this allegiance. How does it deal with this problem?

The structural characteristics of the Nation tend to insulate the member from the hostility of the larger society and thus contribute to the organization's survival. To begin with, the ritual of joining the organization itself stresses commitment without questions.

At the end of the general address at a temple meeting, the minister asks those nonmembers present who are "interested in learning more about Islam" to step to the back of the temple. There they are given three blank sheets of ordinary stationery and a form letter addressed to Elijah Muhammad in Chicago:

Dear Savior Allah, Our Deliverer:

I have attended the Teachings of Islam, two or three times, as taught by one of your ministers. I believe in it. I bear witness that there is no God but Thee. And, that Muhammad is Thy Servant and Apostle. I desire to reclaim my Own. Please give me my Original name. My slave name is as follows:

The applicant is instructed to copy this letter verbatim on each of the three sheets of paper, giving his own name and address unabbreviated at the bottom. If he fails to copy the letter perfectly, he must repeat the whole task. No explanation is given for any of these requirements.

Formal acceptance of his letter makes the new member a Muslim, but in name only. Real commitment to the Nation of Islam comes gradually—for example, the personal commitment expressed when a chain smoker gives up cigarettes in accordance with the Muslim rules even though he knows that he could smoke unobserved. "It's not that easy to do these things," Stanley X said of the various forms of abstinence practiced by Muslims. "It takes will and discipline and time, . . . but you're a much better person after you do." Calvin X told of periodic backsliding in the beginning, but added, "Once I got into the thing deep, then I stuck with it."

This commitment and the new regimen that goes with it have been credited with effecting dramatic personality changes in many members, freeing alcoholics from the bottle and drug addicts from the needle. It can be argued, however, that the organization does not change the member's fundamental orientation. To put it somewhat differently, given needs and impulses can be expressed in a variety of ways; thus, a man may give vent to his sadism by beating up strangers in an alley or by joining the police force and beating them up in the back room of the station.

"Getting into the thing deep" for a Muslim usually comes in three stages:

■ Participation in organizational activities—selling the Muslim newspaper, dining at the Muslim restaurant, attending and helping run Muslim meetings.

■ Isolation from non-Muslim social contacts—drifting away from former friends and associates because of divergent attitudes or simply because of the time consumed in Muslim activities.

■ Assimilation of the ideology—marking full commitment, when a Muslim has so absorbed the organization's doctrines that he automatically uses them to guide his own behavior and to interpret what happens in the world around him.

The fact that the organization can provide a full social life furthers isolation from non-Muslims. Participation is not wholly a matter of drudgery, of tramping the streets to sell the paper and studying the ideology. The organization presents programs of entertainment for its members and the public. For example, in two West Coast cities a Negro theatrical troupe called the Touring Artists put on two plays, "Jubilee Day" and "Don't You Want to Be Free." Although there was a high element of humor in both plays, the basic themes—white brutality and hypocrisy and the necessity of developing Negro self-respect and courage— were consonant with the organization's perspective. Thus the organization makes it possible for a member to satisfy his need for diversion without going outside to do so. At the same time, it continually reaches him with its message through the didactic element in such entertainment.

Carl X's experiences were typical of the recruit's growing commitment to the Nation. When asked what his friends had thought when he first joined, he replied: "They thought I was crazy. They said, 'Man, how can you believe all that stuff?' " He then commented that he no longer saw much of them, and added:

When you start going to the temple four or five times a week and selling the newspaper you do not have time for people who are not doing these things. We drifted—the friends I had—we drifted apart. . . . All the friends I have now are in the Nation. Another Brother and I get together regularly and read the Koran and other books, then ask each other questions on them like, "What is Allah's greatest weapon? The truth. What is the devil's greatest weapon? The truth. The devil keeps it hidden from men. Allah reveals it to man." We read and talk about the things we read and try to sharpen our thinking. I couldn't do that with my old friends.

Spelled out, the "stuff" that Carl X had come to believe, the official Muslim ideology, is this:

■ The so-called Negro, the American black man, is lost in ignorance. He is unaware of his own past history and the future role which history has destined him to play.

■ Elijah Muhammad has come as the Messenger of Allah to awaken the American black man.

■ The American black man finds himself now in a lowly state, but that was not always his condition.

■ The Original Man, the first men to populate the earth, were non-white. They enjoyed a high level of culture and reached high peaks of achievement.

■ A little over 6,000 years ago a black scientist named Yakub, after considerable work, produced a mutant, a new race, the white race.

■ This new race was inferior mentally, physically, and morally to the black race. Their very whiteness, the very mark of their difference from the black race, was an indication of their physical degeneracy and moral depravity.

■ Allah, in anger at Yakub's work, ordained that the white race should rule for a fixed amount of time and that the black man should suffer and by his suffering gain a greater appreciation of his own spiritual worth by comparing himself to the whites.

■ The time of white dominance is drawing near its end. It is foreordained that this race shall perish, and with its destruction the havoc, terror, and brutality which it has spread throughout the world shall disappear.

■ The major task facing the Nation of Islam is to awaken the American black man to his destiny, to acquaint him with the course of history.

■ The Nation of Islam in pursuing this task must battle against false prophets, in particular those who call for integration. Integration is a plot of the white race to forestall its own doom. The black bourgeoisie, bought off by a few paltry favors and attempting to ingratiate themselves with the whites, seek to spread this pernicious doctrine among so-called Negroes.

■ The Nation of Islam must encourage the American black man to begin now to assume his proper role by wresting economic control from the whites. The American black man must gain control over his own economic fortunes by going into business for himself and becoming economically strong.

■ The Nation of Islam must encourage the so-called Negro to give up those habits which have been spread among them by the whites as part of the effort to keep them weak, diseased, and demoralized. The so-called Negro must give up such white-fostered dissolute habits as drinking, smoking, and eating improper foods. The so-called Negro must prepare himself in mind and body for the task of wresting control from the whites.

■ The Nation of Islam must encourage the so-called Negro to seek now his own land within the continental United States. This is due him and frees him from the pernicious influence of the whites.

Commitment to the Nation can diminish as well as grow. Four of the members I interviewed later defected. Why?

These four cases can be explained in terms of a weak point in the structure of the Nation. The organization has no effective mechanisms for handling grievances among the rank and file. Its logic accounts for this. Muslim doctrine assumes that there is a single, ultimate system of truth. Elijah Muhammad and, by delegation, his ministers are in possession of this truth. Thus only Elijah Muhammad himself can say whether a minister is doing an adequate job. The result is the implicit view that there is nothing to be adjudicated between the hierarchy and its rank and file.

Grievances arise, however. The four defectors were, for various reasons, all dissatisfied with Minister Gerard X. Since there were no formal mechanisms within the organization for expressing their dissatisfaction, the only solution was to withdraw.

For most members, however, the pattern is one of steadily growing involvement. And once the ideology is fully absorbed, there is virtually no such thing as dispute or counterevidence. If a civil rights bill is not passed, this proves the viciousness of whites in refusing to recognize Negro rights. If the same bill *is* passed, it merely proves the duplicity of whites in trying to hide their viciousness.

The ideology also provides a coherent theory of causation, provided one is willing to accept its basic assumptions. Norman X interpreted his victory over his wife in a court case as a sign of Allah's favor. Morris X used it to account for the day-to-day fortunes of his associates.

Minister X had some trouble. He was sick for a long time. He almost died. I think Allah was punishing him. He didn't run the temple right. Now the Brothers make mistakes. Everyone does—but Minister X used to abuse them at the meetings. It was more a personal thing. He had a little power and it went to his head. Allah struck him down and I think he learned a little humility.

When a man reasons in this fashion, he has become a fully committed member of the Nation of Islam. His life revolves around temple-centered activities, his friends are all fellow Muslims, and he sees his own world—usually the world of an urban slum dweller—through the framework of a very powerful myth. He is still doing penance for the sins of Yakub, but the millennium is at hand. He has only to prepare.

The Nation of Islam does not in any real sense convert members. Rather it attracts Negroes who have already, through their own experiences in white America, developed a perspective congruent with that of the Muslim movement. The recruit comes to the door of the temple with the essence of his ideas already formed. The Black Muslims only give this disaffection a voice.

December 1966

FURTHER READING SUGGESTED BY THE AUTHOR:

Outsiders: Studies in the Sociology of Deviance, by Howard S. Becker. London: Free Press of Glencoe, 1963. Provides a theoretical framework for analyzing behavior such as joining the Nation of Islam.

Black Nationalism: a Search for an Identity in America, by E. Essien-Udom. Chicago: University of Chicago Press, 1962. Valuable mainly in that it was done by an African.

Putting on
The Youth Opportunity Center

DAVID WELLMAN

In the summer of 1966 I studied a Federal government program designed to help lower-class youths find jobs. The program was known as TIDE. It was run by the California Department of Employment, and classes were held five days a week in the Youth Opportunities Center of West Oakland.

The TIDE program was anything but a success. "I guess these kids just don't want jobs," one of the teacher-counselors told me. "The clothes they wear are loud. They won't talk decent English. They're boisterous. And they constantly fool around. They refuse to take the program seriously."

"But isn't there a job shortage in Oakland?" I asked. "Does it really *matter* how the kids act?"

"There's plenty of jobs. They're just not interested."

The students were 25 young men and 25 young women selected by poverty-program workers in the Bay

Area. Their ages ranged from 16 to 22, and most were
Negroes. The government paid them $5 a day to par-
ticipate. Men and women usually met separately. I sat
in on the men's classes.

The young men who took part in TIDE had a distinctive style. They were "cool." Their hair was "processed." All sported sunglasses—very lightly tinted,
with small frames. They called them "pimp's glasses."
Their clothes, while usually inexpensive, were loud and
ingeniously altered to express style and individuality.
They spoke in a "hip" vernacular. Their vocabularies
were small but very expressive. These young men, as
part of the "cool world" of the ghetto, represent a
distinctively black working-class culture.

To most liberals these young men are "culturally deprived" or "social dropouts." Most had flunked or been
kicked out of school. Few had any intention of getting
a high-school degree. They seemed uninterested in
"making it." They had long and serious arrest and
prison records. They were skeptical and critical of both
the TIDE program and white society in general.

The TIDE workers were liberals. They assumed that
if the young men would only act a little less "cool"
and learn to smooth over some of their encounters with
white authorities, they too could become full-fledged,
working members of society. The aim of TIDE was not
to train them for jobs, but to train them how to *apply*
for jobs—how to take tests, how to make a good impression during a job interview, how to speak well,
how to fill out an application form properly. They
would play games, like dominoes, to ease the pain associated with numbers and arithmetic; they would conduct mock interviews, take mock tests, meet with man-
agement representatives, and tour places where jobs

might be available. They were told to consider the TIDE program itself as a job—to be at the Youth Opportunities Center office on time, dressed as if they were at work. If they were late or made trouble, they would be docked. But if they took the program seriously and did well, they were told, they stood a pretty good chance of getting a job at the end of four weeks. The unexpressed aim of TIDE, then, was to prepare Negro youngsters for white society. The government would serve as an employment agency for white, private enterprise.

The program aimed to change the youngsters by making them more acceptable to employers. Their grammar and pronunciation were constantly corrected. They were indirectly told that, in order to get a job, their appearance would have to be altered: For example, "Don't you think you could shine your shoes?" Promptness, a virtue few of the youngsters possessed, was lauded. The penalty for tardiness was being put on a clean-up committee, or being docked.

For the TIDE workers, the program was a four-week exercise in futility. They felt they weren't asking very much of the youngsters—just that they learn to make a good impression on white society. And yet the young men were uncooperative. The only conclusion the TIDE workers could arrive at was: "They just don't want jobs."

Yet most of the youngsters took *actual* job possibilities very seriously. Every day they would pump the Youth Opportunities Center staff about job openings. When told there was a job at such-and-such a factory and that a particular test was required, the young men studied hard and applied for the job in earnest. The TIDE program *itself,* however, seemed to be viewed as

only distantly related to getting a job. The youngsters
wanted jobs, but to them their inability to take tests
and fill out forms was *not* the problem. Instead, they
talked about the shortage of jobs available to people
without skills.

Their desire for work was not the problem. The real
problem was what the program demanded of the young
men. It asked that they change their manner of speech
and dress, that they ignore their lack of skills and society's lack of jobs, and that they act as if their arrest
records were of no consequence in obtaining a job. It
asked, most important, that they pretend *they,* and not
society, bore the responsibility for their being unemployed. TIDE didn't demand much of the men: Only
that they become white.

What took place during the four-week program
was a daily struggle between white, middle-class ideals
of conduct and behavior and the mores and folkways
of the black community. The men handled TIDE the
way the black community in America has always treated white threats to Negro self-respect. They used subtle
forms of subversion and deception. Historians and
sociologists have pointed to slave subversion, to the
content and ritual of Negro spirituals, and to the blues
as forms of covert black resistance to white mores.

Today, "putting someone on," "putting the hype on
someone," or "running a game on a cat" seem to be
important devices used by Negroes to maintain their
integrity. "Putting someone on," which is used as much
with black people as with whites, allows a person to
maintain his integrity in a hostile or threatening situation. To put someone on is to publicly lead him to
believe that you are going along with what he has to
offer or say, while privately rejecting the offer and

subtly subverting it. The tactic fails if the other person recognizes what is happening. For one aim of putting someone on is to take pride in feeling that you have put something over on him, often at his expense. (Putting someone on differs from "putting someone down," which means active defiance and public confrontation.)

TIDE was evidently interpreted by the men as a threat to their self-respect, and this was the way they responded to it. Sometimes TIDE was put on. Sometimes it was put down. It was taken seriously only when it met the men's own needs.

There was almost no open hostility toward those in charge of TIDE, but two things quickly led me to believe that if the men accepted the program, they did so only on their own terms.

First, all of them appeared to have a "tuning-out" mechanism. They just didn't hear certain things. One young man was a constant joker and talked incessantly, even if someone else was speaking or if the group was supposed to be working. When told to knock it off, he never heard the command. Yet when he was interested in a program, he could hear perfectly.

Tuning-out was often a collective phenomenon. For instance, there was a radio in the room where the youngsters worked, and they would play it during lunch and coffee breaks. When the instructor would enter and tell them to begin work, they would continue listening and dancing to the music as if there were no one else in the room. When *they* were finished listening, the radio went off and the session began. The youngsters were going along with the program—in a way. They weren't challenging it. But they were undermining its effectiveness.

A second way in which the young men undermined

the program was by playing dumb. Much of the program consisted of teaching the youngsters how to fill out employment applications. They were given lengthy lectures on the importance of neatness and lettering. After having filled out such forms a number of times, however, some students suddenly didn't know their mother's name, the school they last attended, or their telephone number.

This "stupidity" was sometimes duplicated during the mock job interviews. Five or more of the students would interview their fellow trainees for an imaginary job. These interviewers usually took their job seriously. But after it became apparent that the interview was a game, many of the interviewees suddenly became incredibly incompetent. They didn't have social-security numbers, they couldn't remember their last job, they didn't know what school they went to, they didn't know if they really wanted the job—to the absolute frustration of interviewers and instructors alike. Interestingly enough, when an instructor told them one morning that *this* time those who did well on the interview would actually be sent out on a real job interview with a real firm, the stupid and incompetent were suddenly transformed into model job applicants.

The same thing happened when the youngsters were given job-preference tests, intelligence tests, aptitude tests, and tests for driver's licenses. The first few times the youngsters took these tests, most worked hard to master them. But after they had gotten the knack, and still found themselves without jobs and taking the same tests, their response changed. Some of them no longer knew how to do the test. Others found it necessary to cheat by looking over someone's shoulder. Still others flunked tests they had passed the day before. Yet when they were informed of actual job possibilities at the naval ship yard or with the post office, they insisted on giving and taking the tests themselves. In one instance, some of them read up on which tests were relevant for a particular job, then practiced that test for a couple of hours by themselves.

Tuning-out and playing stupid were only two of the many ways the TIDE program was "put-on." Still another way: Insisting on work "breaks." The young men "employed" by TIDE were well-acquainted with this ritual, and demanded that it be included as part of their job. Since they had been given a voice in deciding the content of the program, they insisted that breaks become part of their daily routine. And no matter what the activity, or who was addressing them, the young men religiously adhered to the breaks.

The program started at 9:30 A.M. The youngsters decided that their first break would be for coffee at 10:30. This break was to last until 11. And while work was never allowed to proceed a minute past 10:30, it was usually 11:15 or so before the young men actually got back to work. Lunch began exactly at 12. Theoretically, work resumed at 1. This usually meant 1:15, since they had to listen to "one more song" on the radio. The next break was to last from 2:30 to 3. However, because they were finished at 3:30 and because it took another 10 minutes to get them back to work, the fellows could often talk their way out of the remaining half hour. Considering they were being paid $5 a day for five hours' work, of which almost half were regularly devoted to breaks, they didn't have a bad hustle.

Games were another part of the TIDE program subverted by the put-on. Early in the program an instructor told the students that it might be helpful if they mastered arithmetic and language by playing games—dominoes, Scrabble, and various card games. The students considered this a fine idea. But what their instructor had intended for a pastime during the breaks, involving at most an hour a day, they rapidly turned into a major part of the instruction. They set aside 45 minutes in the morning and 45 minutes in the afternoon for games. But they participated in these games during their breaks as well, so that the games soon became a stumbling block to getting sessions back in order after breaks. When the instructor would say, "Okay, let's get back to work," the men would sometimes reply, "But we're already working on our math—we're playing dominoes, and you said that would help us with our math."

To familiarize the students with the kinds of jobs potentially available, the TIDE instructors took them on excursions to various work situations. These excursions were another opportunity for a put-on. It hardly seemed to matter what kind of company they visited so long as the visit took all day. On a trip to the Oakland Supply Naval Station, the men spent most of their time putting the make on a cute young WAVE who was their guide. One thing this tour did produce, however, was a great deal of discussion about the war in Vietnam. Almost none of the men wanted to serve in the armed forces. Through the bus windows some of them would yell at passing sailors: "Vietnam, baby!" or "Have a good time in Vietnam, man!"

The men would agree to half-day trips only if there was no alternative, or if the company would give away samples. Although they knew that the Coca-Cola Company was not hiring, they wanted to go anyway, for the free Cokes. They also wanted to go to many candy and cookie factories. Yet they turned down a trip to a local steel mill that they knew was hiring. TIDE, after all, was not designed to get them an interview—its purpose was to show them what sorts of jobs might be available. Given the circumstances, they reasoned, why not see what was *enjoyable* as well?

When the men were not putting-on the TIDE program and staff, they might be putting them down. When someone is put-down, he knows it. The tactic's success *depends* on his knowing it, whereas a put-on is successful only when its victim is unaware of it.

Among the fiercest put-downs I witnessed were those aimed at jobs the students were learning to apply for. These jobs were usually for unskilled labor: post-office, assembly-line, warehouse, and longshore workers, truck drivers, chauffeurs, janitors, bus boys, and so on.

The reaction of most of the students was best expressed by a question I heard one young man ask an instructor: "How about some tests for I.B.M.?" The room broke into an uproar of hysterical laughter. The instructor's response was typically bureaucratic, yet disarming: "Say, that's a good suggestion. Why don't you put it in the suggestion box?" The students didn't seem able to cope with that retort, so things got back to normal.

Actual employers, usually those representing companies that hired people only for unskilled labor, came to TIDE to demonstrate to the men what a good interview would be like. They did *not* come to interview men for real jobs. It was sort of a helpful-hints-for-successful-interviews session. Usually one of the more socially mobile youths was chosen to play the role of job applicant. The entire interview situation was played through. Some employers even went so far as to have the "applicant" go outside and knock on the door to begin the interview. The students thought this was both odd and funny, and one said to the employer: "Man, you've already *seen* the cat. How come you making him walk out and then walk back in?"

With a look of incredulity, the employer replied: "But that's how you get a job. You have to sell yourself from the moment you walk in that door."

The employer put on a real act, beginning the interview with the usual small talk.

"I see from your application that you played football in high school."

"Yeah."

"Did you like it?"

"Yeah."

"Football really makes men and teaches you teamwork."

"Yeah."

At this point, the men got impatient: "Man, the cat's here to get a job, not talk about football!"

A wisecracker chimed in: "Maybe he's interviewing for a job with the Oakland Raiders."

Usually the employer got the point. He would then ask about the "applicant's" job experience, draft status, school record, interests, skills, and so on. The young man being interviewed usually took the questions seriously and answered frankly. But after a while, the rest of the group would tire of the game and (unrecognized, from the floor) begin to ask about the specifics of a real job:

"Say man, how much does this job pay?"

"What kind of experience do you need?"

"What if you got a record?"

It didn't take long to completely rattle an inter-viewer. The instructor might intervene and tell the students that the gentleman was there to help them, but this would stifle revolt for only a short while. During one interview, several of the fellows began loudly play-ing dominoes. That got the response they were looking for.

"Look!" shouted the employer. "If you're not inter-ested in learning how to sell yourself, why don't you just leave the room so that others who are interested can benefit from this?"

"Oh no!" responded the ringleaders. "We work here. If you don't dig us, then *you* leave!"

Not much later, he did.

Sometimes during these mock interviews, the very nature of the work being considered was put-down. During one mock interview for a truck-driving job, some of the men asked the employer about openings for salesmen. Others asked him about executive posi-tions. At one point the employer himself was asked point-blank how much he was paid, and what his ex-perience was. They had turned the tables and were enjoying the opportunity to interview the interviewer. Regardless of a potential employer's status, the young men treated him as they would their peers. On one tour of a factory, the students were escorted by the vice-president in charge of hiring. To the TIDE partici-pants, he was just another guide. After he had in-formed the students of the large number of unskilled positions available, they asked him if he would hire some of them, on the spot. He replied that this was just a tour and that he was in no position to hire anyone immediately. One youth looked at him and said: "Then you're just wasting our time, aren't you?"

Although shaken, the executive persisted. Throughout his talk, however, he innocently referred to his audience as "boys," which obviously bothered the students. Finally one of the more articulate men spoke up firmly: "We are young *men,* not boys!"

The vice-president blushed and apologized. He made a brave attempt to avoid repeating the phrase. But habit was victorious, and the word slipped in again and again. Each time he said "you boys" he was corrected, loudly, and with increasing hostility.

The students treated State Assemblyman Byron Rumford, a Negro, the same way. The meeting with Rumford was an opportunity for them to speak with an elected official about the job situation in the state. The meeting was also meant to air differences and to propose solutions. At the time, in fact, the men were quite angry about their rate of pay at TIDE. An instructor had suggested that they take the matter up with Rumford.

The meeting was attended by both the young men and women in the TIDE program. The young women were very well-dressed and well-groomed. Their clothes were not expensive, but were well cared for and in "good taste." Their hair was done in high-fashion styles. They looked, in short, like aspiring career women. The young men wore their usual dungarees or tight trousers, brightly colored shirts and sweaters, pointed shoes, and sunglasses.

The women sat quietly and listened politely. The men spoke loudly whenever they felt like it, and constantly talked among themselves.

Rumford, instead of speaking about the job situation in the Bay Area, chose to talk about his own career. It was a Negro Horatio Alger story. The moral was that if you work hard, you too can put yourself through college, become a successful druggist, then run for public office.

The moment Rumford finished speaking and asked for questions, one of the men jumped up and asked, "Hey man, how do we get a raise?" A male chorus of "Yeah!" followed. Before Rumford could complete a garbled answer (something like, "Well, I don't really know much about the procedures of a federally sponsored program"), the battle of the sexes had been joined. The women scolded the men for their "disrespectful behavior" toward an elected official. One said: "Here he is trying to help us and you-all acting a fool. You talking and laughing and carrying on while he talking, and then when he finishes you want to know about a raise. Damn!"

"Shit," was a male response. "You don't know what you talking about. We got a *right* to ask the cat about a raise. We elected him."

"We supposed to be talking about jobs," said another. "And we're talking about *our* job. If y'all like the pay, that's your business. We want more!"

The debate was heated. Neither group paid any attention to Rumford, who wisely slipped out of the room.

During the exchanges it became clear to me that the differences in clothing and style between the sexes reflected their different orientations toward the dominant society and its values. In the minds of the young women, respect and respectability seemed paramount. At one point, a young woman said to the men, "You acting just like a bunch of *niggers.*" She seemed to identify herself as a Negro, not as a "nigger." For the men, on the other hand, becoming a Negro (as opposed to a "nigger") meant giving up much that they considered positive. As one young man said in answer to the above, "You just ain't got no soul, bitch."

The women's identification with the values of white society became even clearer when the debate moved from what constituted respect and respectability to a direct attack on a personal level: "Do you all expect to get a job looking the way you do?" "Shit, I wouldn't wear clothes like that if I was on welfare."

The direction of the female attack corresponded closely with the basic assumptions of the TIDE program: People are without jobs because of themselves. This barrage hit the young men pretty hard. Their response was typical of any outraged male whose manhood has been threatened. In fact, when one young woman gibed, "You ain't no kinda man," some of the fellows had to be physically restrained from hitting her.

One of the men explained that "maybe the reason cats dress the way they do is because they can't afford anything else. Did you ever think of that?"

The woman's response was one I had not heard since the third or fourth grade: "Well, it doesn't matter what you wear as long as it's clean, pressed, and tucked-in. But hell, you guys don't even shine your shoes."

The battle of the sexes in the black community seems to be almost a class conflict. Many observers have noted that the black woman succeeds more readily in school than the black man. Women are also favored by parents, especially mothers. Moreover, the black woman has been for some time the most stable force and the major breadwinner of the Negro family. All these things put Negro women in harmony with the major values attached to work and success in our society. Black men, however, have been estranged from society, and a culture has developed around this estrangement—a male Negro culture often antagonistic to the dominant white society. The black woman stands in much the same relation to black men as white society does.

Even including Rumford, no group of officials was put down quite so hard as the Oakland police. Police brutality was constantly on the youngsters' minds. A day didn't pass without at least one being absent because he was in jail, or one coming in with a story about mistreatment by the police. A meeting was arranged with a sergeant from the Community Relations Bureau of the Oakland police. The students seemed excited about meeting the officer on their own turf and with the protection provided by the program.

In anticipation of his arrival, the fellows rearranged the room, placing all the separate tables together. Then they sat down in a group at one end of the table, waiting for the officer.

Sergeant McCormack was an older man. And while obviously a cop, he could also pass for a middle-aged businessman or a young grandfather.

"Hi boys," he said as he sat down. His first mistake. He began with the five-minute speech he must give to every community group. The talk was factual, uninteresting, and noncontroversial: how the department is run, what the qualifications for policemen are, and how difficult it is for police to do their work and still please everyone. His talk was greeted with complete silence.

"I understand you have some questions," McCormack finally said.

"What about police brutality?" asked one man.

"What is your definition of police brutality?" the sergeant countered.

"How long you been a cop?" someone shouted.

"Over 20 years."

"And you got the nerve to come on sounding like you don't know what we talking about. Don't be jiving us. Shit, if you've been a cop *that* long, you *got* to know what we talking about."

"Righteous on that, brother!" someone chimed in.

"Well, I've been around a while, all right, but I've never seen any brutality. But what about it?"

"What *about* it?" There was a tone of disbelief mixed with anger in the young man's voice. "Shit man, we want to know why you cats always kicking other cats' asses."

The officer tried to draw a distinction between necessary and unnecessary police violence. The fellows weren't buying that. They claimed the police systematically beat the hell out of them for no reason. The officer asked for examples and the fellows obliged with long, involved, and detailed personal experiences with the Oakland Police Department. The sergeant listened patiently, periodically interrupting to check details and inconsistencies. He tried to offer a police interpretation of the incident. But the fellows were simply not in a mood to listen. In desperation the sergeant finally said, "Don't you want to hear *our* side of the story?"

"Hell no, motherfucker, we *see* your side of the story every night on 14th Street."

One young man stood up, his back to the officer, and addressed his contemporaries: "We *tired* of talking! We want some action! There's a new generation now. We ain't like the old folks who took all this shit off the cops." He turned to the sergeant and said, "You take that back to your goddamn Chief Preston and tell him."

McCormack had a silly smile on his face.

Another youngster jumped up and hollered, "You all ain't going to be smiling when we put dynamite in your police station!"

The officer said simply, "You guys don't want to talk."

"You see," someone yelled, "the cat's trying to be slick, trying to run a game on us. First he comes in here all nice-talking, all that shit about how they run the police and the police is to protect us. And then when we tell him how they treat us he wants to say we don't want to talk. Shit! We want to talk, he don't want to listen."

From this point on, they ran over him mercilessly. I, with all my biases against the police, could not help feeling compassion for the sergeant. If the police are an authority figure in the black community, then this episode must be viewed as a revolt against authority— *all* authority. There was nothing about the man's life, both private and public, that wasn't attacked.

"How much money you get paid?"

"About $12,000 a year."

"For being a cop? Wow!"

"What do you do?"

"I work in the Community Relations Department."

"Naw, stupid, what *kind* of work?"

"I answer the telephone, speak to groups, and try to see if the police treat the citizens wrong."

"Shit, we could do that and we don't even have a high-school education. Is that all you do? And get that much money for it?"

"Where do you live?"

"I'll bet he lives up in the hills."

"I live in the east side of Oakland. And I want you

to know that my next-door neighbor is a colored man. I've got nothing against colored people."

"You got any kids?"

"Yeah, two boys and a girl."

"Shit, bet they all went to college and got good jobs. Any of your kids been in trouble?"

"No, not really."

"What do they do?"

"My oldest boy is a fighter pilot in Vietnam."

"What the hell is he doing over there? That's pretty stupid."

"Yeah man, what are we fighting in Vietnam for? Is that your way of getting rid of us?"

"Well, the government says we have to be there and it's the duty of every citizen to do what his country tells him to do."

"We don't want to hear all that old bullshit, man."

"Hey, how come you wear such funny clothes? You even look like a goddam cop."

"Yeah baby, and he smells like one too!"

The barrage continued for almost half an hour. The instructor finally called a halt: "Sergeant McCormack has to get back, fellows. Is there anything specific that you'd like to ask him?"

"Yeah. How come Chief Preston ain't here? He's always talking to other people all over the country about how good the Oakland cops are and how there ain't going to be no riot here. Why don't he come and tell us that? We want to talk with the chief."

The next day, Deputy Chief Gain came—accompanied by the captain of the Youth Division, the lieutenant of that division, and a Negro sergeant. It was a formidable display of police authority. The youngsters were noticeably taken aback.

Chief Gain is a no-nonsense, businesslike cop. He takes no static from anyone, vigorously defends what he thinks is correct, and makes no apologies for what he considers incorrect. He is an honest man in the sense that he makes no attempt to cover up or smooth over unpleasant things. He immediately got down to business: "All right now, I understand you guys have some beefs with the department. What's the story?"

The fellows started right in talking about the ways they had been mistreated by the police. The chief began asking specific questions: where it happened, when it happened, what the officer looked like, and so on. He never denied the existence of brutality. That almost seemed to be assumed. He did want details, however. He always asked whether the youth had filed a complaint with the department. The response was always No. He then lectured them about the need to file such complaints if the situation was to be changed.

He explained the situation as he saw it: "Look fellows, we run a police force of 654 men. Most of them are good men, but there's bound to be a few rotten apples in the basket. I know that there's a couple of men who mistreat people, but it's only a few and we're trying our best to change that."

"Shit, I know of a case where a cop killed a cat and now he's back on the beat."

"Now wait a minute—"

"No more waiting a minute!" someone interrupted. "You had two cops got caught taking bribes. One was black and the other Caucasian. The black cat was kicked off the force and the white cat is back on."

"Yeah, and what about that cat who killed somebody off-duty, what about him?"

"Hold on," Gain said firmly. "Let's take these things

one at a time." He didn't get very far before he was back to the "few rotten apples" argument.

"If it's only a few cops, how come it happens all the time?"

The deputy chief told them that he thought it was the same few cops who were causing all the problems. "Unless you file complaints each time you feel you've been mistreated, we can't do anything about it. So it's up to you as much as it is up to us."

For the first time in weeks, I intruded into the discussion. I pointed out to Gain that he was asking citizens to police their own police force. He had argued that in most situations the department had a good deal of control over its own men—the same argument the police had used against a civilian-review board. Now he was saying the opposite: that it was up to the citizens. This seemed to break the impasse, and the students howled with delight.

"What happens if a cop beats my ass and I file a complaint?" demanded one. "Whose word does the judge take?"

"The judge takes the evidence and evaluates it objectively and comes to a decision."

"Yeah, but it's usually two cops against one of us, and if both testify against me, what happens? Do you think the judge is going to listen to me?"

"Bring some witnesses."

"That ain't going to do anything."

"That's your problem. If you don't like the legal system in this country, work to change it."

"Okay man," one fellow said to Gain, "You pretty smart. If I smack my buddy here upside the head and he files a complaint, what you gonna do?"

"Arrest you."

"Cool. Now let's say one of your ugly cops smacks *me* upside the head and I file a complaint—what you gonna do?"

"Investigate the complaint, and if there's anything to it, why we'll take action—probably suspend him."

"Why do *we* get arrested and *you* investigated?"

The deputy chief's response was that most private companies with internal difficulties don't want to be investigated by outside agencies. The fellows retorted: "Police are *not* a private business. You're supposed to work for the people!"

"And shit, you cats get to carry guns. No businessman carries guns. It's a different scene, man."

"How come you got all kinds of squad cars in this neighborhood every night? And have two and three cops in each of them?"

"The crime rate is high in this area," replied Gain, "and we get a lot of calls and complaints about it."

"Yeah, and you smart enough to know that when you come around here, you better be wearing helmets and carrying shotguns. If you that clever, you got to be smart enough to handle your own goddamn cops.

At this point the fellows all jumped on the deputy chief the same way they had jumped on the sergeant the day before:

"Why don't you just let us run our own damn community?"

"Yeah. There should be people on the force who've been in jail because they the only people who know what it means to be busted. People in West Oakland should be police because they know their community; you don't."

"Why do we get all the speeding tickets?"

"How come we got to fight in Vietnam?"

"Why the judges so hard on us? They don't treat white cats—I mean dudes—the way they do us."

The chief began assembling his papers and stood up. "You guys aren't interested in talking. You want to yell. When you want to talk, come down to my office and if I'm free we'll talk."

But the fellows had the last word. While he was leaving they peppered him with gibes about how *they* were tired of talking; promised to dynamite his office; and called the police chief a coward for not coming down to speak with them.

When the deputy chief had gone, the instructor asked the fellows why they insisted on ganging up on people like the police. The answer provides a lot of insight into the young men's actions toward the police, businessmen, and public officials:

"These people just trying to run a game on us. If we give them time to think about answers, they gonna put us in a trick. We've *got* to gang up on them because they gang up on us. Did you dig the way that cat brought three other cats with him? Besides, how else could we put them down?"

In effect, the young men had inverted the meaning and aims of the TIDE program. It was supposed to be an opportunity for them to plan careers and prepare themselves for their life's work. The immediate goal was to help them get started by showing them how to get a job. The youngsters had a different view. The program was a way to play some games and take some outings—an interesting diversion from the boredom and frustration of ghetto life in the summer. In some respects it was also a means of confronting, on equal terms, high-status people normally unavailable to them—and of venting on them their anger and hostility. But primarily they saw it as a $5-a-day job.

The program simply did not meet the needs of these young men. In fact, it was not really meant to. The Great Society was trying to "run a game on" black youth. TIDE asked them to stop being what they are. It tried to lead them into white middle-class America by showing that America was interested in getting them jobs. But America does not provide many jobs— let alone attractive jobs—for those with police records, with few skills, with black skins. The youths knew that; TIDE workers knew that, too. They did not train youths for work, but tried to make them believe that if they knew *how* to get a job, they could. The young men saw through the sham.

Ironically, the view that Negro youths, rather than society, are responsible for the employment problem is very similar to the familiar line of white racism. Negroes will not work because they are lazy and shiftless, the old Southern bigot would say. The Northern liberal today would put it a little differently: Negroes cannot get jobs because of their psychological and cultural impediments; what they need is cultural improvement, a proper attitude, the ability to sell themselves. Both views suggest that inequities in the job and opportunity structure of America are minor compared to the deficiencies of Negroes themselves. In the end, Northern liberals and Southern racists agree: The problem is mainly with Negroes, not with our society. This fallacy underlies much of the war on poverty's approach and is indicative of the subtle forms racism is taking in America today.

April 1968

Black Culture
Or Lower-class Culture

BENNET BERGER

Behind much of the recent trouble within the civil rights
movement there lurks the seldom-asked question about the
reality of a distinctive Negro culture. The split in the
movement over the black power slogan reveals publicly for
the first time just how profound that question is. The work
of the NAACP and other moderate civil rights groups has
emphasized the use of the law to achieve for individual
Negroes their full rights as ordinary citizens, but these
organizations have shown little interest in the ethnic character of Negro group life. The recent emphasis of the
more militant sectors of the Negro revolution has been to
claim for Negroes more than just their rights as individual
citizens of a United States whose laws do not generally
recognize subcultures. What we are now seeing in the
Negro revolution, with its growing emphasis on racial or
ethnic "pride" and "identity" (as well as on voting, housing,
and job rights), is an attempt to *legitimize* black culture

117

and to claim for it full parity with the rest of America's ethnic styles.

If this development has raised the specter of "racism in reverse," it is partly because of intentional distortions by those who, for whatever reason, wish to obstruct Negro gains. But it is partly, too, a result of the apparent reticence the leaders of the black left have shown so far in stating concretely what patterns of black American culture they are affirming and wish preserved. For if the affirmation of black culture carries with it no clear specification of the *culture* being affirmed, it is less than surprising that middle-class people (already full of anxieties and apprehensions) should fear that it is simply blackness (or its mystique) which is being celebrated. Black culture—and its political slogan, black power—is a troublesome perspective for the Negro movement, then, because it may alienate white liberals and because it may lose the movement the support of the middle classes, white and black. But also once the radicals invoke the perspective and the rhetoric of black culture, they place themselves under the intellectual obligation to concern themselves with clarifying precisely *what* patterns of Negro culture they are affirming, *what* sources of institutional support for these patterns they see in Negro social organization, and *how* those patterns may be expected to provide the bases of "racial pride" and "ethnic identity" sufficient to motivate the black masses to claim both their full rights as Americans *and* the nation's respect for their ethnicity.

The importance of Charles Keil's *Urban Blues* is that it is the best of very few books to attempt some answers to these questions. Keil sketches the history and structure of the blues as a musical form, describes its relevance to the social role of the blues singer or "bluesman" in Negro society, and analyzes the relation of black culture to the problems that Negroes face in American society. It seems to me that the questions to which Keil addresses himself are so crucial—particularly to the present problems of the civil rights movement and the future of Negroes in the United States—that it is more important to say that he has made a brilliant start than to say that his book has important flaws which prevent one from praising it wholeheartedly.

Keil's basic thesis, emblazoned by his publisher on the dust jacket of the book, is that Negroes are "the only substantial minority group in America who really have a culture to guard and protect . . . and a unique perspective by incongruity on American society that may be this nation's outstanding and redeeming virtue." The distinctiveness of black culture extends, according to Keil, from its religious institutions (the ecstatic character of the store front churches), to its kinship institutions (the female-based household and the elusive, uncertain character of the Negro male role in it), to its distinctive sense of time and history (drift, living in the present), to its distinctive modes of perception and expression (auditory and tactile rather than visual and literary). This culture is manifest in the lyrics of the blues, in the status of the bluesman and other hustlers (preachers, comedians, entertainers—anybody, as Keil puts it, talented enough and clever enough to be financially well off without working) who "tell it like it is," and in the emergence of the "soul" ideology as the expression of a nativist, revitalization movement.

Keil traces the blues to their African sources but goes much further than the usual romanticizers of "earthy" Negro music to an analysis of the blues in terms of its textures (instrumentation, tonality, etc.), structures (rhythmic and verbal patterns), lyrics, and contexts (the geographical circumstances in which these are shaped). From these concepts he develops a typology of blues styles, ranging in an ascending order of sophistication from "country" to "city" to "urban" to a contemporary mixed style of "soul" music. In doing this he does not bother to conceal his contempt for the "moldy fig" mentality of blues historians (usually white) whose image of a "real" blues singer demands that he be aged, blind, arthritic, and toothless, having lived most of his life sharecropping, coaxing mules, and picking cotton, and preferably not having performed in public or made a record in 20 years. His contempt extends not only to this image, which he sees as a liberal's version of the white man's burden, but also to the overly genteel blues historian for whom "a coarse lyric of 30 years ago has poetic qualities and historical interest," but for whom the same sort of contemporary lyric is "frivolous and not worthy of scholarly attention."

Learned in ethnography as well as musicology, Keil makes a genuine *research* contribution to the understanding of these matters not just through his historical command of the sources but through chapters which describe the business context in which a blues singer gets his start, through depth interviews with blues singers and their audience, through a marvelous blow-by-blow report of the intensifying development of rapport and solidarity between audience and performers at a large blues dance-concert in Chicago, the center of the contemporary blues renaissance, and through the use of a radio call-in show on a Negro station to evoke responses from listeners regarding the meanings they ascribe to the concept of "soul." But impressive and original as this research is, his conclusions about the blues are less important than the inferences he makes from them about the character of black culture and the role of bluesmen in it.

"If we are ever to understand what urban Negro culture

is all about, we had best view entertainers and hustlers as culture heroes." For Keil, bluesmen (and, to an extent, other hustlers—especially preachers) are *ritual* performers whose audiences are mostly "committed" rather than "appreciative" (as they are, say, in the *art* music that modern jazz has become). What these audiences want most from their ritual performers is what they call "soul"—that is, the projection of authenticity of feeling about a subject matter that concerns them all (salvation and other religious matters in the preacher's case; sex, prison, gambling, whiskey, and the rest of the common coin of ghetto life in the case of the bluesman) and that permits a sort of vicarious identification and collective catharsis. These performers function as culture or opinion leaders whose talent it is to tell it, if not quite like it is, then like their inarticulate audiences feel it to be—a function, incidentally, which links the bluesman and his audience to the rock and roll groups and their teen audience.

In the context of black culture it is this quasi-sacred, expressive role which relates the bluesman to the preacher and even to some extent to the political leader. They are all, as Keil says, "identity experts" whose performances are significant less for any objective technical or aesthetic merit they may possess (although they may possess plenty) than for their common function of stirring collective response in their audiences in reminding them of their common identity as a people. Keil makes brilliant observations about the *stylistic* parallels, many-rooted African traditions, between bluesmen and preachers (observations whose validity extends even to the political rhetoric of leaders like Malcolm X and Stokely Carmichael)—for example, the repetition of phrases, the incantatory quality of utterance, and the use of shouts and falsettos.

He makes these observations without at the same time

losing sight of the important cultural differences between bluesmen and preachers. For of all hustlers, the preacher is just about the only role model of a "good man" black culture contains. The preacher is good because in addition to soul he's got responsibility, whereas the bluesman and other hustlers more directly involved in entertainment represent the "no-good man," that model of Negro masculinity with a strong sex-role identity as stud, rogue, or lady-killer, the exigencies and uncertainties of whose work render him here today but perhaps gone tomorrow. In short, the bluesman is a good lover but a bad husband and provider. But his functional kinship with the preacher helps explain what Keil reports as a distinct tendency for bluesmen to *become* preachers when their careers in show business are over.

It is Keil's involvement with and affirmation of the blues culture which leads him to see these things so clearly. But his involvement and affirmation begin to mislead him, I think, when he ascribes not simply a diffuse emotional charisma but a specifically political charisma to urban bluesmen who, he says, sense broader and deeper obligations to their people than country and city bluesmen. He cries plenty of evidence, for example, for his suggestion that the style and lyrics of urban blues state common problems clearly and concisely, but cites none at all for his assertion that they also take steps toward the analysis and solution of these problems, except, perhaps, for his assertion that the ritual aspects of blues performance contribute to the establishment of racial solidarity—which the left wing of the civil rights movement apparently regards as essential to any further political gains.

Borrowing an idea from LeRoi Jones, Keil sees Negro music becoming more "reactionary" (more African) in recent years as white America appropriates and commercializes more and more Negro music. As this occurs, the "black community" generates a "new" music it can call its own—as Keil puts it, a black equivalent of white backlash: " . . . The soul brothers seem to be saying: 'Let us fight for our rights . . . because we value our cultural identity and wish to be able to develop it without fearing punishment from the white majority.' " There is a strong nativistic quality to this black revitalization movement, but it is very complex too, and Keil recognizes this all too well. He understands that the affirmation of black experience (from Africa through the slavery and ghetto experience) can function as something to fall back on if the civil rights movement fails and American realities become too grim to cope with. But Keil sees too that many of the most militant spokesmen for black culture may be less interested in integration than in freedom and self-respect because they have vested ethnic interests in that culture (as black barbers, undertakers, and insurance men have vested economic interests in segregation) which may make them reluctant to risk disappearance in the white mainstream.

But in spite of this sophistication, Keil is misled by the sort of faith and commitment which, although they honor him as a man, distort his intellectual judgment. He gives himself away, for example, when, in a book characterized most of the way by close observation and careful reason, he says that even after ghetto conditions are remedied, "Negroes will cherish their cultural identity and see in their 'entertainers' the carriers of an irreplaceable tradition which they will be unwilling to cast aside for middle class anonymity." The statement looks at first glance as if it might be a reasoned prediction when it is actually nothing more than a statement of faith and hope which flies in the face of what is by now persuasive evidence to the contrary. It seems clear enough, indeed Keil has helped *make* it clear enough, that the blues culture emerged out of slavery and the ghetto experience and that the blues have changed in response to changing conditions. Keil gives one no grounds for believing in the probability of their surviving the ghetto very long—other than his observation that because they deal with conflict between the sexes the blues are not likely to disappear. Even if the ghetto remains, it is not likely to remain as a homogeneous slum but as a complexly stratified subsociety in which even urban blues are likely *not* to reflect the experience of a substantial part of that society as different segments of it begin to move, at varying rates, out of leaden-eyed poverty into the discontents of ordinary citizenship.

Keil is mislead on this point by what I think is a need to affirm his solidarity with black people. And this need blunts the force of his own considerable analytical powers —ironically, because I think those powers are released by his actual detachment, perhaps even alienation. Thus he is led to overcompensate with rhetorical flourishes such as "I will continue to dispute those who insist that Negroes have no worthwhile culture," a statement which, like the one quoted in the previous paragraph, is nothing more than platform oratory to which the only plausible responses are a cheer or a shrug. The important issue with respect to the civil rights movement and the future of Negroes in the United States is less whether he or I or you dig black culture than it is for us to understand the quality of that culture, its function in the lives of the black masses who affirm it (to the *extent* that they do—itself an unanswered question), and to appraise the prospects of its survival when the conditions which generated it and sustain it are no longer present.

The essential quality of that culture is summarized by the concept of soul, which Chicago Negroes defined for Keil and his disc-jockey collaborator with phrases such as: strong emotions and feelings, especially when shared with others; something pure, nonmachined; staying power and wisdom through suffering; telling it like it is, being what you are, and believing in what you do. The concept suggests further a tight intermingling of sex, love, and reciprocal responsiveness which constitute the pattern of Negro Dionysianism, manifest in the swing of the blues-jazz-gospel musical milieu and in the brilliant, moving, linguistic innovations which spring from it. The pattern emphasizes the erotic, the frenetic, and the ecstatic—a pattern which when made ideological constitutes a claim to emotional depth and authenticity (the special cultural heritage possessed by black Americans and by those few whites, like Tony Bennett and Frank Sinatra, who come by the gift mysteriously).

This idea is a stereotype which, like all stereotypes, is founded in fact and, like some stereotypes, seems to flatter the group supposedly characterized by it. But it is hard for any group, particularly an oppressed one, to resist the stereotypes which apparently flatter it, especially when, for reasons one is never fully able to anticipate, such stereotypes not only serve the interests of the flatterers but also mollify the people stereotyped who may be unaware that such mollification may confirm them in the cultural patterns which help perpetuate their oppression. So now to the cleverness of the Jews and the blarney-charm of the Irish and the fire of the Latins we are asked to add the soul of the Negroes.

As an attribute of "race," such a stereotype is of course

nonsense. To the extent that the soul idea is founded in fact, it may be partly African in origin; it is certainly partly Southern rural and perhaps partly evangelical Christian, but it is mostly lower class. As ideology, it is part of a venerable intellectual tradition which has characterized the lower class (and some other oppressed groups) in terms not very different from those emotionally hot-cool terms in which Keil describes black culture. Since the eighteenth century (if not earlier) those relegated to the bottom of the social heap have been heir to a ready-made ideology which contrasted their .own vigor, vitality, and authentic humanity with the repressions, the desk-boundness, and the futile status-seeking of the successful. This ascription of greater energy, sexuality, and emotional attunedness to the oppressed and the exploited than to the pale, thin, bloodless, beardless pencil-pushers who inhabit the offices of the world was one of the few small comforts granted the downtrodden, serving them as a palliative for their actual discontents, and serving their intellectual spokesmen as a symbol of their redemptive potential.

But the soul ideology does not suit that probably enormous number of Negroes who would gladly trade a piece of their abundant emotionality for a piece of American affluence and who care less about having an "authentic" and "worthwhile" culture than about having a good job and a house in the suburbs. To those Negroes who already have these or are on the verge of getting them, soul may well be experienced as a symbol of a sort of old country culture in which they are pressured to participate and to which they are constrained to respond with real feeling when in fact it may be losing or already have lost most of its meaning for them. The danger is that having or not

having soul may be invoked as a sort of test of ethnic
loyalty and used as weapon in a campaign of slander against
those guilty of the crime of mobility. By whom? By those
Negro leaders who, having given priority to the political
goals of racial pride and ethnic identity over the goal of
integration, might be tempted to seek support for these
priorities by characterizing the already integrated or the
almost integrated as having sold their souls for a piece of
the American pie, or, as Keil puts it, for "middle-class
anonymity."

Keil's ambivalence shows here, since what he says he
actually hopes for from the revitalization of black culture
is the production of a race of marginal men (like Marx,
Freud, or Einstein) whose grapplings with conflicting identities shape a mind which is skeptical and inquiring instead
of one which, having suppressed conflict, assimilates and
then is helpless when the bigots march. But Keil has not
shown how racial solidarity will contribute to this goal.
Of all ideologies, racial and ethnic ones tend to be intol-
erant of marginality or of anything less than full commitment. Moreover any political gains to be had from "racial
solidarity" must be balanced against losses in support—not
simply from white liberals, but from those Negroes who
still hope for a comfortable place in an integrated, middle
class America. For stripped of its mystique, black culture
is basically an American Negro version of *lower-class culture,* and, race prejudice aside, it can expect *on this ground
alone* to meet strong resistance from the overwhelming
majority of the American population which will see in the
attempt to legitimate it an attempt to strike at the heart
of the ethic of success and mobility, which is as close as
this country comes to having any really sacred values. No
lower-class culture has ever been fully legitimated in the

United States because the basic right of members of the lower class has been to rise out of it but not to celebrate its style of life!
June 1967

Black Culture:
Lower-class Result
or Ethnic Creation?

ROBERT BLAUNER

*This is the original (summer 1967) draft stimulated by the
review of Bennett Berger which precedes it in this volume.
Professor Berger himself, in a rare expression of the community of scholarship, as well as others, notably Charles
Keil, Lawrence Levine, and Lee Rainwater, provided
searching criticisms of this draft. Their comments were
helpful in preparing a revised version which appears as
"Black Culture: Myth or Reality?" in* Afro-American Anthropology, *Norman Whitten and John Szwed, editors,*
The Free Press, Macmillan Company, 1969, *and in* Americans From Africa, *Peter Rose, editor, Atherton Press, 1969.
I have left the present essay essentially as originally written
despite current reservations about a number of points. For
example, I have come to agree with my critics Charles Keil
and Huey P. Newton that Afro-American culture is not
weak. Rather, this culture lacks clarity and unity, due to the
sociological factors I have tried to analyze below. In addi-*

tion I am not satisfied with the concept of neoracism; and am presently attempting to think through the confusions and ambiguities in the present formulation. I should also add that this essay was written before the publication of Harold Cruse's The Crisis of the Negro Intellectual *(1967) and* Rebellion or Revolution *(1968); therefore I could not benefit from his wealth of seminal ideas.*

In their communities across the nation, Afro-Americans are discussing "black culture." The mystique of "soul" is only the most focused example of this trend in consciousness. What is and what should be the black man's attitude toward American society and American culture is becoming a central division in the Negro protest movement. The spokesmen for black power celebrate black culture and Negro distinctiveness; the integrationists base their strategy and their appeal on the fundamental "American-ness" of the black man. There are nationalist leaders who see culture-building today as equal or more important than political organization. From Harlem to Watts there has been a proliferation of black theater, art, and literary groups; the recent ghetto riots (or revolts as they are viewed from the nationalistic perspective) are favored materials of these cultural endeavors. The spread of resistance to the draft and the Vietnam war seems to indicate an increasing tendency among blacks to reject certain basic values of American life. But as with so many of these apparent "tendencies", it is difficult to know whether this one portends an actual change in sentiment or instead reflects the new conditions that have lifted some of the past inhibitions against its expression.

The emergence of this cultural revitalization movement among American Negroes poses a number of dilemmas for the larger society. There are the problems of practice and policy for the institutions of education, welfare, politics, and their professional and administrative representatives. There is also an intellectual dilemma for the analysts of American society and its culture. The black culture movement flies in the face of certain basic assumptions upon which social scientists and liberal intellectuals have constructed the nation's official "enlightened" attitudes toward race relations and the Negro minority. The primary tenet is that Negroes—unlike other minority groups—have no ethnic culture because the elimination of African ancestral heritages brought about total acculturation. A second related assumption posits the distinctiveness of the ghetto subculture to *lower-class* conditions rather than to ethnic or national traditions. The middle-class character and mobility goals of most federal antipoverty efforts follow from this tenet. The present essay is addressed to these contradictions. I attempt to make sense of today's cultural ferment in the black communities by questioning the standard sociological position on the ethnic character of Afro-Americans.

The view that Negroes lack any characteristics of a distinctive nationality, that they are only Americans and nothing else has become standard dogma of liberal social science. Gunnar Myrdal and his great study *An American Dilemma* set the tone for the present outlook. In this influential and otherwise voluminous work there is no chapter on Negro cultural orientations and the briefest treatment of the black community. Furthermore, Myrdal's statement that the Negro is "an exaggerated American" and that his values are "pathological" elaborations on general American values have been widely quoted for a generation. In the introduction to *The Peculiar Institution,* published in 1956, the historian Kenneth Stampp asserted that Negroes are

"white men with black skins," even though his thorough
scholarship raises troubling questions about his statement.
And as recently as 1963, Glazer and Moynihan repeated the
Myrdal position when they wrote "the Negro is only an
American and nothing else. He has no values and culture
to guard and protect."

It is misleading to give the impression that the "official
position" reflects only the vantage point of the white liberal
sociologist. E. Franklin Frazier has been at least as influential as Myrdal in gaining acceptance for this outlook.
Frazier entered the debate in an effort to counter the ex-
tremism of Melville Herskovits who in his *Myth of the
Negro Past* imputes African origins to many, if not most,
Negro American social and cultural patterns. Frazier's
view was published as late as 1957 in the revised edition of
his comprehensive work, *The Negro in the United States:*

> As a racial or cultural minority the Negro occupies a
> unique position. He has been in the United States longer
> than any other racial or cultural minority with the
> exception, of course, of the American Indian. Although
> the Negro is distinguished from other minorities by his
> physical characteristics, unlike other racial or cultural
> minorities the Negro is not distinguished by culture
> from the dominant group. Having completely lost his
> ancestral culture, he speaks the same language, practices
> the same religion, and accepts the same values and poli-
> tical ideals as the dominant group. Consequently, when
> one speaks of Negro culture in the United States, one
> can only refer to the folk culture of the rural Southern
> Negro or the traditional forms of behavior and values
> which have grown out of the Negro's social and mental
> isolation. Moreover, many of the elements of Negro cul-
> ture which have grown out of his peculiar experience

in America, such as music, have become a part of the general American culture.

Since the institutions, the social stratification, and the culture of the Negro minority are essentially the same as those of the larger community, it is not strange that the Negro minority belongs among the assimilationist rather than the pluralist, secessionist or militant minorities. It is seldom that one finds Negroes who think of themselves as possessing a different culture from whites and that their peculiar culture should be preserved.

When Negro sociologists present community studies of Southern towns and Northern ghettoes, however, they describe distinctive institutions, and unique ways of looking upon life and society that begin to read like the depiction of an ethnic culture. Yet until recently the positive assertion of Negro culture has been confined to nationalist and political circles; it has not been defended through analysis and evidence in the academic field. This is what makes *Urban Blues* by Charles Keil an important book. Keil, a white anthropologist, uses the blues singer and his audience as the raw materials to outline the distinctive traits and ethos of Afro-American culture. He finds the core of this culture in the "soul" ideology. Soul may be related to the more archetypal "wisdom-through-suffering" theme, but as Keil pieces it together, it suggests "that Negroes have a dearly bought experiential wisdom, a 'perspective by incongruity,'" that provides black Americans a unique outlook on life that cannot be shared by whites.

Keil's rich study, to which I shall return later, stimulated an incisive critical review by the sociologist Bennett Berger. In the context of general admiration for Keil's achievement, Berger attacks his major thesis at three pivotal points. First, he asserts that "soul" theorists like Keil in their romanticization of Negro life miss the key fact that "black culture" is at bottom only an American Negro version of lower-class culture. Second, analytical appreciation of this culture may be misplaced since it has no future. Lower-class culture in America is no basis for the development of a national consciousness and ethnic solidarity. Since it will have no appeal to the socially mobile, it can only get in the way of progress toward integration and equality. Third, this suggests for Berger that black culture spokesmen are only confusing the intellectual atmosphere and obstructing the road to Negro progress and racial harmony. As intellectuals and political men, they have the obligation to clearly specify what in Negro culture is to be affirmed, so that we all can see whether anything solid or meaningful is involved. But speaking so generally if not demagogically they fail to do so.

The various positions discussed, from Myrdal to Frazier to Berger, share in common the idea that American Negroes have no ethnic culture. The first formulation asserts that black culture is American culture, the second and more recent positions argue that Negro orientations are Southern-regional or lower-class. I suggest that this approach is based on a number of misconceptions about culture and ethnicity in modern American society. It reflects first a narrow usage of the culture concept, but more importantly the mechanical application of the model of immigrant ethnic group assimilation to the deviant cultural process of the black man. Second, it is a response to the confusion and complexity of Negro American culture which stems from its many contradictory sources as well as a refusal to credit the prime role of racism—and its residues, Negro political history—in that cultural process. Finally, it is based on a static, deterministic approach to cultural development, an approach which minimizes its open-ended quality and therefore underplays the role of consciousness and culture-building in affecting that development. Let us examine each of these issues in turn.

The Unique Cultural Process

There is a sociological plausibility to the argument that Negroes are only Americans with black skins. As Frazier stressed, the manner in which North American slavery developed—in contrast to Caribbean and South American slavery—eliminated the most central African traits, those elements of ethnicity which European and Asian immigrants brought to this country: language, dress, religions, and other traditional institutions, a conscious identification with an overseas homeland. Basic as is this critical difference, it misses the point in assuming that there is only one generic process—that model of European ethnic assimilation through which nationality cultures and the dominant American ethos have interacted. What must be understood is the uniqueness of the Negro American condition, an essential aspect of which has been a deviant cultural experience that to some degree is the reverse of those of the traditional ethnic minorities.

Howard Brotz has observed that the "no Negro culture" argument rests on the assumption that an ethnic group must possess three attributes: a distinctive language, a unique religion, and a national homeland. This position is also tied to the anthropologist's classical concept of culture, a usage that is less applicable to the condition of any ethnic group in modernized mass society. This is the *holistic* view of culture, which points to the integrated way of life, that system of customs, institutions, beliefs and values that fit together into some organic whole, perhaps dominated by a central ethos. This concept was of course developed from the study of primitive peoples. Yet it fairly well captures the unity of the social heritages that the various immigrant groups brought to America. The parallel holistic cultures of the African peoples were destroyed in America because slaves from the diverse tribes, kingdoms, and linguistic groups were consciously separated so that language, religion, and national loyalties were soon lost. But ethnic cultures as organic, holistic ways of life did not last very long either for the immigrant nationalities. Today when we characterize Jews, Italians or Greeks as ethnic groups, we are referring implicitly to a different notion of culture. This is the idea that the ethnic culture resides in a certain number of distinctive values, orientations to life and experience and shared memories that co-exist within the framework of the general American life-style and allegiances. Most sociologists and laymen find little difficulty in calling American Jews an ethnic group despite the fact that in most of their institutional and cultural behavior, Jews are nothing if not American and middle class. But there are also distinctive cultural orientations, a peculiarly ethnic style in humor for example, that came from a common historical and social experience.

Let us look more closely at the model of ethnic group assimilation that dominates sociological thinking about national cultures. The holistic way of life was introduced at the outset of the immigrant group's entry, or more accurately, early in the peak periods of its immigration. It soon gave way to the demands of the American environment and the competition of American ways of life. Typically after one generation an ethnic culture developed that combined old country and American ways, that was more fragmented and full of normative and value conflicts than the traditional culture, and yet still provided some round of life and center of community for the group. As

time went on, the numbers of people in each group involved in the more traditional holistic culture declined,
and the emerging ethnic-American culture tended to take
on more and more characteristics of the larger society.
Assimilation meant the modification or the giving up of
certain ethnic institutions and culturally distinct values as
the generations followed one another. Though life experience may have been incredibly subtle and complex,
the sociological model that captures the immigrants cultural experience is fairly simple. There are basically two
variables, the traditional culture and the American values
and conditions. The process tends to be a one-way, non-
reversible one, from immigrant extra-national status to
ethnic group to assimilation, though Herberg and others
have noted a tendency to reassert ethnic identity in the
third generation. The means that move this process forward are occupational mobility and the ethnic's increasing
contact with dominant institutions, especially education.

Very little of this fits the cultural experience of Afro-
Americans. How a minority group enters the host society
has fateful—if not permanent—consequences. The very
manner in which Africans became Americans undermined
traditional culture and social organization. The black man
did not enter this country with a group identity as a Negro.
This group category could only be formed by the slave-
making operation which vitiated the meaning and relevance
of the traditional, specific African identities. Therefore
the cultural process could not be one of movement from
ethnic group to assimilation, since Negroes were not an
ethnic group. What took place first was a kind of too
quick and too-total absorption without the group autonomy,
social and economic equality that was the concomitant of
assimilation for other minorities. But at the same time,

beginning with slavery, the group and culture-building process began among the black population, and the development of an ethnic group identity and distinctive culture has been going on ever since. But this cultural process is infinitely more complex than that of the immigrant ethnic groups. One reason is the general reversal in direction. But it is not a simple one-way process in the opposite direction, from "assimilation" to ethnic group. The black cultural experience more resembles an alternating current than it does a direct current. The movement toward ethnicity and distinctive consciousness has been paralleled by one of becoming more "American" in action and identity. Sometimes these conflicting vectors characterize different time periods; sometimes they reflect different segments of the large and diversified black minority: but in addition these contradictory cultural tendencies have taken place simultaneously and within the psyches and social orientations of the same individuals. Behind all this are the many and various historical and social conditions that have produced Negro American culture. Black culture therefore cannot be understood in terms of the simplified two-variable model which is reasonably satisfactory for the ethnic groups.

The Many Sources of Negro American culture

The present essay will not attempt to characterize the contents of black culture. As I see it, this is a difficult if not impossible job for a white social scientist in today's America. The job will be eventually done by the more appropriate workmen in this jurisdiction, the Negro intellectuals and sociologists. Furthermore, it is my estimate that black culture is at present too much in flux for a systematic schematization to have much value. My task rather is to make some broad generalizations about the conditions in American life that have and are presently giving rise to distinctive Negro American cultural orientations. Central to my argument against the official liberal intellectual position is the thesis that the *ghetto subculture involves both lower-class and ethnic characteristics.* Poverty is only one source of black culture, and as I shall attempt to prove, even the lower class traits and institutions in Negro life have been modified by strictly ethnic values. Among the other sources of black culture are Africa, slavery, the South, Emancipation and Northern migration, and above all, *racism.* That racist oppression provides the basis for a more elaborate and more ethnic cultural response than does class exploitation and lower class status is a central postulate of the present thesis.

Afro-American culture is an ethnic as well as a class culture because the history of black people in the United States has produced a residue of shared collective memories and frames of reference. It is because black Americans have undergone unique experiences in America, experiences that no other national or racial minority or lower-class group have shared, that a *distinctive* ethnic culture has evolved. Though this culture is overwhelmingly the product of American experience, the first contributing source is still African. Herskovits undoubtedly exaggerated the power of African continuities, but it seems plausible that some aesthetic and linguistic principles that underline Negro-American music and dialect (as well as possible some movement patterns and religious orientations) have their origins in those peoples, tribes, and kingdoms that furnished the slave trade. However, the importance of African patterns for American Negro ethnicity was greatly reduced by the fact that these orientations had to be transmitted largely on the subliminal level rather than that of conscious awareness and identification. Recently of course, with the emergence of independent African nations, a concern with this continent has become more prominent in the cultural symbolism of the black community and presumably also in the personal identities of many individual Negroes.

The first great source of black culture in America is slavery. Here under seriously restricting conditions, American Negroes began developing their own quasi-communities and their own codes of conduct. Here certain prevailing patterns such as ecstatic religion, mother-led families, anti-white attitudes, and the yearning for freedom and autonomy got their start. More negative adaptations and character-types, for example, the submission, timidity, fear and manipulation embedded in the "Uncle Tom" orientation, also owe their origins to slavery. It is these kinds of cultural adaptations that many nationalist leaders are trying to stamp out in their attacks on "the slave mentality."

Related to slavery as a second great source of Negro ethnicity is the subculture of the American South. Ralph Ellison and more recently Calvin Hernton have pointed out how much of the black man's attitudes and cultural styles reflect the patterns of this region. Much (but not all) of Negro religion, "soul food," and language is similar to poor-white counterparts. But the black man also assimilated some of the values and the style of the Southern ruling classes, though he was not always in a position to emulate them. Ellison has attributed the general aristocratic flavor of ghetto life-styles to this origin, as well as the American Negro's apparent lack of passion for business entrepreneurship.

A further source was Emancipation: the promises, the betrayals, and the frustrations that followed upon release from servitude. There may be much in Negro American patterns that still reflects a "freedman's culture"; I refer to the great mobility, the moving about and restlessness that characterizes the life patterns of an important minority (especially male) within this great minority group. This mobility, the promise of the North, the attractions of industry, and the push from a depleted Southland, set the stage for ghetto life in the urban North. This is the source of black culture which is most clearly tied to poverty and lower-class existence. And yet the Negro ghetto is different from the ethnic ghettos of the Irish, Jews or Chinese because it comes out of a different history, that of slavery, Southern Jim Crow, and northern migration rather than from a transoceanic search for a better life. *It is also different in its cultural impact because it exists in a racist society which makes no serious move to assimilate black Americans.* For this reason the Negro ghettos have served more as the setting for the flowering of a distinctive ethnicity, whereas the immigrant ghettos were actually way-stations in the process of acculturation and assimilation.

The lower-class component. The black ghettos are overwhelmingly made up of low-income people, and poverty is the first fact of life. This has naturally encouraged the view that the ghetto subculture is lower-class culture, or the "culture of poverty" to use Oscar Lewis' now fashionable phrase. This interpretation is based upon the liberal assumption that Negro Americans lack distinctive ethnic or national characteristics and on the social science discovery that lower-class groups in America share a way of life and somewhat deviant orientations that we call a subculture. Since black Americans are overwhelmingly in the low-income population, whatever appears to be distinctive in the ghetto culture must be due to class status rather than ethnicity.

In *Urban Blues,* the most exhaustive, serious treatment of Negro American culture up to now, Keil does not deal explicitly with the analytical problem of class and ethnic contributions. Working with the blues as his chief material, he identifies the ideology and behaviors associated with "soul" as the keystones of that culture. Bennett Berger, on the other hand, in his interesting review, bases his argument on the theory that ghetto culture is essentially lower-class in character. I think Berger finds Keil's overplaced emphasis (from my viewpoint) on "soul" very convenient to his position since this real and yet elusive cultural symbol of black America does contain many of the values, orientations, and virtues that have been historically attributed to the poor and downtrodden. As Berger (drawing from Keil) summarizes "soul", it has become the stereotype that flatters the oppressed Negro lower class and thus can serve as a compensation, an ideological palliative for its discontents:

... strong emotions and feelings, especially when shared with others; something pure, non-machined; staying power and wisdom through suffering; telling it like it is, being what you are, and believing in what you do. The concept suggests further a tight intermingling of sex, love, and reciprocal responsiveness which constitute the pattern of Negro Dionysianism, manifest in the swing of the blues-jazz-gospel musical milieu and in the brilliant, moving, linguistic innovations which spring from it. The pattern emphasizes the erotic, the frenetic, and the ecstatic—a pattern which when made ideological constitutes a claim to emotional depth and authenticity ...

As this capsule summary suggests, there are many themes in ghetto life that can be identified in other lower-class groups, for example the Latin American poor described by Lewis or the immigrant ghettos of the Irish and the Poles. Some of these themes are a present-oriented and expressive style of life, characterized by minimal planning and organization. Religion is usually a more dominant value and release than politics; crime, hustling, rackets, and other forms of "deviance" are commonplace. Economic pressures strain the family, and matriarchal trends are visible. Aggression and violence are more frequent occurrences than in middle-class neighborhoods. Expressive personal releases that some sociologists label "immediate rather than deferred gratifications"—sex, drinking, drugs, music— are emphasized in the life organization of individuals. A sense of fatalism, even apathy or quasi-paranoid outlooks, the "world is against me," pervades the streets, where the public life of the lower-class subculture is set.

That the black ghetto shares these cultural traits with other lower-class milieux and that these themes flow primarily from the condition of poverty I do not doubt. But that is not the whole story. Even the class characteristics gain an ethnic content and emphasis when people with unique problems live under similar conditions and associate primarily with one another for generations. The expressiveness of Negroes is more articulated and developed than the expressiveness of lower-class Poles, for example. Not only music, but language, styles of dress and movement also are more consciously cultivated. The religion of Southern blacks has similar institutional origins as that of Southern whites, but as Powdermaker observed in the 1930's, a Negro church service is a totally different happening than a poor-white one.

Berger is correct in his observation that lower-class traits do not become institutionalized or legitimated. But when class traits are modified and given ethnic content by a national group, they may become institutionalized, that is conscious, expected, and infused with value (which can be positive or negative). The developing ethnicity of black Americans long ago infused value into its folk music; the same is being done today for its Southern rural cuisine, modes of walking and talking, and even its alleged "super-sexuality." (The development of ethnic cultural values does not preclude of course ambivalence; the fact that many people may feel ambivalent toward these phenomena is no argument against their cultural reality. Just the contrary!) My argument can perhaps be best illustrated by the matri-archy controversy. Though some reactions to the "Moynihan report" may suggest otherwise, black people are well aware that for centuries the mother has played a more dominant role in the Negro family and community than she does in the larger society. Unlike the situation with lower classes in which the matrifocal theme generally operates amid a value system that stresses patriarchy and therefore obscures the detection and confrontation of this trend, Negroes *expect* to see women playing independent and powerful roles. Since the matriarchy is a conscious and expected reality, it is talked about, joked about, defended against, debated pro and con, and more and more actively acted upon, for example in selecting the leadership of community antipoverty boards and other political groups. It is be-coming more and more infused with negative value. This type of cultural ferment in the black communities is not characteristic of lower classes, nor even of organized work-ing classes in America. It indicates a dynamic of self-definition through which an ethnic group is coming into existence.

The class and ethnic factors in Negro American culture are so intimately intermingled that they are very difficult to distinguish. The effort must be made, however, because the intellectual and social consequences of this apparently innocent distinction are considerable—as I shall suggest in my concluding section.

Perhaps the critical reader might agree that slavery, emancipation, and the Southern heritage are a unique constellation that no other lower-class minority group shared. Yet, these great events are more than 100 years past, and the Southern element is dying out as the South itself changes. There is still much in the Northern ghettos today that resembles the life conditions of the ethnic immigrants. All this is true and it might shatter my argument except for one fact. *A continuing racist social structure has served to consolidate rather than to erase the distinctive experience of the past.* There is no other lower-class group in America's pluralistic society that has met in the past or meets in the present the systematic barriers of categorical exclusion, blockage, and discrimination based on race and color. This has been such an omnipresent reality for Negroes that the direct and indirect struggle against racism is the core of the history of the Negro group in this country, just as the way in which each black individual has confronted the patterns of exclusion and denigration remains the central theme of his or her personal biography. It is through this continuing struggle to surmount and change a racist social system—a struggle which began at least with Emancipation, and has stepped up to new levels each generation after periods of decline up to the zenith of the present day—that black Americans have created a *political history.* This political history is the core of the emerging ethnic culture, and the clue to the contemporary revitalization movement which celebrates blackness.

In this present period of rapid change, it is often difficult for whites to accept the unpleasant fact that America remains a racist society. Such an awareness is also obscured by the fact that more sophisticated, subtle and indirect forms, that might better be termed neoracism, tend to replace the traditional, open forms that were most highly elaborated in the old South. By American racism, I refer to two key characteristics of our social structure. First, that the division based upon color is the single most important split within the society, the body politic, and the national psyche. Second, that various processes and practices of exclusion, rejection, and subjection based on color are built into the major public institutions (labor market, education, politics and law enforcement) with the effect of maintaining special privileges, power, and values for the benefit of the white majority.

Racism is not only a central though subterranean theme of American culture; its attitude toward black cultures has had from the beginning a profound impact on the course of Negro ethnicity. Initially it alienated its slave population from African culture. It continued its destructive and exploitative sway through the tendency to appropriate and use for profit the cultural creations of Negro Americans: jazz has been the classic example here, but the present day use of ghetto language is in the same vein. Finally in today's more liberal (neoracist) phrase, the official ideology denies the legitimacy, or even the existence, of these subcultural values that make up the black man's distinctive culture.

American racism was the key condition that encouraged a black culture. There are several related reasons for this. First, it blocked the full participation of Negroes in the dominant culture so that unfilled needs for symbols, meaning, and value had to be met elsewhere. Second, Negroes have perceived the fact (as Hernton has recently made explicit) that racism is not an American aberration, but an institution built into the society and its cultural values. In order to protect their selfhoods, black men had to at least partly distance themselves from this culture (if not outright reject it), as the possibilities for assimilation and acculturation in certain areas opened up. Thus again, countervalues and symbols were necessary. (Of course many blacks did not distance themselves and thereby suffered intense inner conflict.) Third, racism made inevitable and necessary group struggles to transform it as a social system and individual efforts to transcend its crippling effects on life, liberty, and the pursuit of opportunity. This century-long battle against racism has created a legacy—the political history of Negroes within the United States. This shared political history is the solid core, the hard-rock nonmystical aspect of Negro American culture.

A unique political history plays an essential role in the development and consolidation of ethnic groups, as well as nations. For the Irish-American community in the late 19th and early 20th century, Ireland's struggle against England and the heroes of this national movement were at the center of ethnic group values and concerns. As others have pointed out, the Jews may be the purest example of a group that has institutionalized its political history into culture, ritual, and sacred values. The Old Testament depicts the political vicissitudes of the Jewish nation and the religious holidays memorialize this milennial struggle for liberation. Perhaps then the attempt of many black nationalist groups to memorialize the death of Malcolm X as an "official" holiday can be understood as a similar recognition of the relation between political history and national culture.

The content of the Negro Americans' political history is beyond the scope of this essay. It is clear, however, that in the past decade, there has been a significant change in the

intensity and nature of this history—a change which lies
behind the present day ferment and renaissance of black
culture. In the past the Negro masses—like the lower
orders of all colors and nations in most eras—were primarily passive politically, acted upon more than acting.
After the 1954 Supreme Court decision (the last major
turning point in American race relations that was initiated
by an act of a "white" institution), blacks have become the
primary active agents for change with respect to the nation's
social structure. Since the mid-fifties Negroes have created
the big news in domestic American history. (Berger notes
that moderate civil rights groups like the NAACP do not
accept the notion of a distinctive Negro culture. By ap-
pearing to limit black culture to the "soul" complex and
ignoring political history, he misses the point that they
have willy-nilly played a part, and an important one, in
developing this culture.)

But important as the decade is, it does not exhaust the
contents of Negro political history that makes black
culture a real sociological phenomenon rather than a
group myth. Despite the fateful reciprocity of black and
white in America (a theme that has been stressed in the
essays of Baldwin and the fiction of W.M. Kelley), Negroes
share a consciousness of a common past (and a concomitant
national or ethnic identification) that white Americans
simply are not privy to. How could whites perceive, react
and relate to slavery, emancipation, to the South and its
history of Jim Crow and lynching, to early 20th century
race riots, and even to Montgomery and Watts in the same
way as blacks? No matter how democratic our ideals and
how sensitive our human capacities, we were on the other
side sociologically and existentially.

The point that I am laboring has been made most succintly

by a reflective blues singer, Al Hibbler. When Charles Keil asked him what it takes to make a soul singer, Hibbler listed three ingredients, "having been hurt by a woman," "being brought up in that old-time religion," and "knowing what that slavery shit is all about." In a nutshell, this is the essence of the Negro's distinctive political history that lies behind the autonomy of his ethnic culture—since no white American can really know "what that slavery shit is all about." Hibbler, of course, was not referring only to the past.

The black man's unique social-political experience also lies behind the other elements of Negro culture that have been recently stressed. The "soul" orientation can be discussed in its Dionysian aspects which emphasize its relation to poverty and lower-class status as Berger does. But it can also be looked at as a philosophy of life or world view that places tragedy, suffering and forebearance in a more central position than does the dominant American ethos. The construction of an orientation toward inner experience that clashes with the more external instrumental orientation of our industrial culture reflects as much the racism that has excluded Negroes from American life as it does lower-class status per se.

Another contribution of racism to Negro American culture is the prominence of *survival* as a focal concern in the black community. The preoccupation with survival is worth examining because of its remarkable salience and because it seems once again simply to reflect the conditions of poverty and lower-class status. What do I mean by the "survival theme"? For one thing, it is very common for black people to express group pride through the argument that the white race would not have survived had we been subject to the past or present life conditions of American Negroes. This sense of tough resilience is one of the central themes in the blues and in the mystique of soul. In the ghetto there is consensus that the problem of every individual is "making it"; "How you makin' it, man," is a common form of greeting. Interviews I have conducted in the Negro community suggest that "making it with dignity" is central to a leading concept of manhood. Finally on the political level, black leaders are becoming concerned with the problem of group survival; a number of "Black Survival Conferences" have been convened on the West Coast.

Poverty and lower-class existence per se also make survival an inevitable and insistent preoccupation. But the Negro American's self-conscious concern with survival and "making it" only reflects in part economic subsistence needs. When black people talk about surviving, they are even more pointedly referring to the problem of maintaining life, sanity, and dignity in a racist society. The backdrop of the "making it" imagery is the presence of the Klan, lynch mobs, ghetto police, and the closed, restricted white power and economic structures. "Making it" appears to be a response to poverty and blocked economic opportunities, but "making it with dignity" is the response of a suppressed national group with their distinctive ethnic (read human) values to defend. Here I refer to the more subtle pressures of white institutions to make Negroes "Tom," smile, or fit conventional stereotypes, or more commonly today, to the pressures to change in middle-class ways that acceptance and success seem to require. Rightly or wrongly, these constraints are interpreted as forms of racism. The survival fears of the black politicos (which incidentally are commonly met among ordinary people in the ghettos today) are not directed at economic poverty. Rightly or wrongly again, they sense a racist plot to eliminate the black population is behind the birth-control efforts aimed at Negro welfare clients, the Vietnam war and its draft policies, and even the alleged readying of concentration camps for ghetto rioters.

The gist of my argument in this section is that racist social relations have different cultural consequences than class relations, and therefore black culture cannot be forced into the Procrustean bed of lower-class culture in the way that Marxists at one time and some liberal social scientists today want to reduce race relations to class relations. For several centuries in America, blacks have lived together in ways that are markedly different than the ways in which lower and working classes live together. This is largely because the manner in which Negroes have been compelled to relate to individual whites and to the larger society is so divergent from the typical relations of the lower classes to the middle classes or to that of the proletariat to a capitalist social order. Racism excludes a category of people from participation in society in a different way than does class hegemony and exploitation. Racism insults, attempts to violate dignity and to degrade personalities in a much more pervasive and inclusive way than class exploitation—which in the U.S. at any rate has typically not been generalized beyond the "point of production." Racist oppression attacks men and manhood more directly and thoroughly than does class oppression. For these reasons racist and class oppression—while intimately interacting—still have diverse consequences for group formation, for the salience of identities based on these groups and for individual and group modes of adaptation and resistance. Class exploitation does not per se stimulate ethnic and national cultures and liberation movements; imperialism, colonialism and domestic racism do.

Oscar Lewis has recently noted that there is a complementary and conflicting relation between the culture of poverty and ethnic group cultures. The classical lower-class culture characterized by apathy, social disorganization, aggression, sexuality and other themes, lacks strong ethnic as well as organized political traditions. When an ethnic culture is viable or when political working class consciousness is cultivated (as Lewis believes has taken place among the Cuban poor), the culture of poverty with all its negative and problematic effects declines. If Lewis is correct—and he makes sense to me—the black culture movement among American Negroes may represent the strengthening of ethnic consciousness, the ethnic cultural component, at the expense of lower-class culture. This strikes me as something that liberal social scientists and intellectuals would want to applaud and appreciate rather than bewail.

Culture-Building and Its Present-Day Role

That Negroes possess an ethnic culture—which is still in the process of development—does not make them less American, though it conditions their relation to American life in distinctive ways. There is no question but that the society's prevailing standards have been a major if not an overwhelming influence on ways of life in the black community. Precisely because black men were stripped of their traditional culture, language and institutions, they were more vulnerable than other groups to American values. But since Negroes could never share fully and participate as equals in that way of life, they assimilated American values from a unique perspective, that of the outsider. As many writers have pointed out, the black population never bought the big myths of America, no matter how much they desired their realization. Certainly Negro culture is American in that it accepts the desirability of money and the material accoutrements of affluence, probably even the suburban life-style. But there is a distinctive ethnic strain in the awareness of the social costs of these goods, in the sensitivity to the hypocrisy in American public and private life, to the gap between the ideal and reality. This long-term awareness appears to be changing into a more outspoken and outright rejection of American middle-class values by at least a substantial (though unknown) number of young Afro-Americans today.

There is a remarkable paradox here in the phenomenon of Negro Americans more actively rejecting the society and its values at the very time when that social order has begun to open its doors to their participation. To some degree and in some cases this may be a "defense mechanism," a protection against the anxieties of openness, competition, and new possibilities. But from another point of view, the paradox is resolved if we understand the peculiarities of the Negro cultural experience set forth in the first section of this essay. In contrast with the situation of the immigrant ethnics, the period of integration and potential assimilation for Negroes is coinciding with the upsurge of the group's sense of peoplehood and with the institutionalization of its culture, rather than with the decline of these phenomena. The Afro-American with mobility and integration chances is therefore torn in a deeper and more profound sense than was the "marginal man" second immigrant generation. The conflict is also greater because the black culture which is now gaining power and clarity is still by all measures a weak culture.

The relative weakness of this culture also helps explain why the existence of a Negro American *ethnic* (as opposed to the lower-class ghetto) culture has been easily dismissed by social scientists and policy-makers. Its traditions, values and patterns of social organization are not as firm as were those of the immigrant nationality groups. The black culture that has emerged has grown out of the soil of American life, and the time in which cultural evolution has been possible is relatively brief—perhaps a hundred years. In addition our social structure does not easily provide the physical isolation and autonomy for groups to develop their own distinctive ways of life (only people like the Amish who have been able to isolate themselves in self-contained and economically sufficient rural pockets have shown quick results in ethnic development). On the one hand, America in its racist dimension excludes the black man and maintains the ghettoized communities that provide the groundwork for Negro ethnicity; with the other hand America in its inclusive, mass homogenizing dimension beckons black men and all others to identify with its material and ideal symbols and to participate in at least the middle levels of consumption and life-styles. This duality and the fact that Afro-American culture has so many diverse sources also contributes to its relative weakness. Compared once again to the immigrant groups upon which sociological models of ethnic group assimilation were built, the Negro is an extremely large and highly differentiated minority. At the high points of immigrant ethnicity, most of these groups were small, their members concentrated in one or more cities and socially in the lower classes. During the periods that black culture has been building up (including the present) the Negro minority continues to differentiate itself. The middle classes grow; new political and religious movements proliferate (e.g., the Muslims); the black population spreads out more evenly across the country—though predominantly now in the urban centers. The development of an ethnic culture moves on at an uneven pace. New values and styles are born and institutionalized in the Northern ghettos at the same time the Southern-originated values and styles lose their hold on many people. There is yet a final reason why Negro American culture appears weaker than it actually is. Blacks have learned to respond to racist depreciation and opportunistic cultural appropriation by concealing many of their deeply held patterns from the white world. White America therefore has not been prepared to respond to any affirmation of black culture beyond the conventional and usually racist stereotypes. We are hearing so much about "soul" today because this old adaptation is dying as a new mood of pride motivates cultural spokesmen to celebrate rather than to deny black values.

That Negro American culture, for many good sociological reasons, may be a relatively weak culture does not mean it is nonexistent. Nor are the black radicals necessarily misguided or visionary in their efforts to strengthen and consolidate it. For it is precisely this deviant, paradoxical character of black culture that makes it especially critical for the group formation and personal identity needs of its bearers. The immigrant ethnic groups had a strong and holistic traditional culture; this gave them an implicit strength and bargaining power in the game of assimilation and acculturation. They had something deep inside the group and individual to fall back upon in the event the American staircase became blocked or its climb too perilous. But the black man has faced the American colossus with an original culture that was shattered. And most important, racism is more profound in its destructive impact on personal identity than was the prejudice and discrimination leveled against the non-black outlanders.

Of course the present cultural ferment in the Negro community is not a totally new thing. Well known is the Harlem renaissance of the 1920's which saw the emergence of a group of self-conscious black intellectuals and artists, along with a somewhat parallel nationalist development in the political field, that of the Garvey movement. This earlier cultural renaissance came after the post-World War I setbacks to racial democratization, just as today's cultural movement gains its power from the limited successes and possibilities of the civil rights movement—specifically the failure of integration to become a social-economic reality. But if culture-building feeds on "backlash," this does not mean it is a temporary will-of-the-wisp that will die out when integration finally hits its stride. The very successes and social legitimation of the civil rights experience of the last ten years has taught some whites what most blacks have probably always known—that racism is not a dying phenomenon in American life, confined largely to decadent Southern elites and their redneck allies. Unfortunately it is only on the way out in these more blatant forms. In various and subtle ways, racism and neoracism permeate the social institutions of society—North, South, West, and East. Thus the black culture movement is a reasonable response to the realities of a society and a people that—as they are at present organized in socioeconomic and psychic structures—are not going to accept Negroes as full human beings without imposing ceilings on their possibilities to reach "the heights of a man." The stronger that Negro ethnic culture becomes, the greater the possibility for black people to utilize *both* group power and individual mobility to take what they can and give what will be accepted from this basically racist society—a process that in time will contribute to the transformation of this society and its racism. For in American life, ethnic culture is identity, and there is no individual or group progress without a clear sense of who one is, where one came from and where one is going.

The black consciousness and culture-building movements

of today seem much more significant than the earlier Harlem development, though this can only be an impressionistic guess for a nonhistorian. Today's movement is more widespread; it is taking place in every major ghetto, not just New York. It encompasses large segments of the black bourgeoisie and working-class masses, rather than primarily marginal people and intellectuals. The appeal of black culture seems *especially* strong today to the occupationally and socially mobile, a group which in the past tended to resist ethnic identification.

Berger, however, in the preceding paper, argues that the soul ideology cannot meet the needs of the upwardly mobile integrationist. It is, he asserts, a lower-class mystique, and they are moving into the middle classes. I think that Berger is dead wrong on this point. Even in America, people cannot live by bread (or television) alone. The mobile young blacks of today seem to be seizing upon the soul concept (and the related black power ideal) because they provide bulwarks of identity and identification in the face of the very anxieties of mobility and assimilation into American life with its cultural emptiness. My recent research and interviewing of community organizers and young college students from low-income ghetto origins suggests that this is so. Certainly, as Berger suggests, there may be new pressures to conform to militant postures and nationalist identifications in order to avoid charges of selling or copping out. But the external pressure point is overemphasized when the need is so intrinsic. This may be why there is more active support for the black-power radicals (as well as for the Muslims) from the mobile Negroes, rather than from the "stable" lower classes in the ghetto. This again seems to reflect a change. A generation ago middle-class Negroes reputedly rejected jazz, blues, gospel music and all other signs of lower-class and Southern roots. Today I find that middle-class black youth keep their car radios tuned in to the soul music stations and switch them on automatically whether riding with whites or blacks.

The young and the youthful are of course at the forefront of the black culture and black power movements. If Claude Brown is correct, E. Franklin Frazier may have had much to do with this generational change in the outlook of the "black bourgeoisie." Brown mentions that Frazier's lectures and his *Black Bourgeoisie* had a great impact on his own thinking, and presumably those of other college students. Of course there is a sense in which these mobile black youth did not have to be motivated to become different from their parents, since in America all young people are predisposed to reject their elders and break away from their life patterns. But in so clearly dissecting the group-denying and the self-negating hangups of their parents, Frazier also helped teach the young generation to identify with their own blackness and with the oppressed ghetto masses. Many of these middle-class college-educated youth have taken on the task of attempting to organize politically, as well as to articulate self-consciously, the less conscious cultural values of the lower-class black man.

Berger's criticism of the Negro cultural "radicals" is probably representative of much white liberal and intellectual thinking on this matter. It is important to understand why he is presumptuous in his complaint that "once the radicals invoke the perspective and rhetoric of black culture, they place themselves under the intellectual obligation to concern themselves with clarifying precisely *what* patterns of Negro culture they are affirming, *what* sources of institutional support for these patterns they see in Negro social organization, and *how* these patterns may be expected to provide the basis of 'racial pride' and 'ethnic identity' sufficient to motivate the black masses to claim both their full rights as Americans *and* the nation's respect for their ethnicity." First he is asking the black intelligentsia to do for their subculture what American social scientists have not adequately accomplished for the society as a whole. The concept of culture—as well-taught undergraduates should know—is a very sticky and troubling concept. There is much scholarly controversy and uncertainty with regard to its essential features. American culture, further, is a most vague and amorphous reality: it simply cannot be pinned down as neatly and conveyed to us as graphically as the ethnographer can capture the culture of a tribal people. This may be partly because we are all caught up in it; more probably it reflects the diversity, the contradictions, and even the weakness of meaning systems and of central patterns in American life. Finally as we have seen, Afro-American culture is an even more complex reality.

Berger has every right not to accept the key assumptions of the black-power movement; here we differ politically and I respect these differences. But he should at least be listening to what these men are saying, for one premise is most central to his pointed criticism of their "failings." As Carmichael reiterates and expresses personally in his dealings with the mass media, one of the essences of black power is self-definition. This means that Negroes select the time, place and manner in which to reveal their plans and strategies outside their own group. Self-definition implies that whites no longer can demand that Negroes do this or that; they have an intellectual obligation to communicate with us only if they choose to become part of our general intellectual community, and for many, the present mood is to choose otherwise. But Berger misses the boat when he implies that black intellectuals are not striving for whatever clarity and specificity that is possible in the present situation. Ralph Ellison has long been calling for such an approach to the Negro cultural experience; conferences where such issues are hammered out have been taking place all over the country recently. But this has become an in-group matter; most of these meetings have been closed to white people. Berger is probably right that such discussions and clarification are essential for the cultural and political dynamics of the Negro movement today; I suspect many black leaders agree with him thus far. But we are not going to hear what is happening until they are good and ready. His demand (and there are many who would voice similar ideas) is out of order because our long-used behind the scenes cartes blanches have expired for sociological voyeurs like Berger and myself.

The demand that Negro spokesmen give us the low-down once and for all on black culture so that we can define our attitude towards it overlooks a reality that is more profound than the new nationalist definition on inter-group relations. It reflects a static approach to social and cultural reality. It assumes that Negro culture is *all there,* or all determined, needing only to be fully detected so the chaff can be separated from the wheat. On the contrary, Negro culture is *in process*, it is a dynamic, open-ended phenomenon, and that is why it is becoming such a central concern of the protest movement. On the basis of the culture that has already been built up out of the American experience of the until recently relatively dormant, silent folk masses, a more self-conscious and explicit national culture is in the process of development. This birth requires the synthesis of the orientations of the ghetto masses with the articulations of the intellectual and political leaders. The middle classes and the marginal people are playing a crucial part as enunciators and systematizers of this nascent culture. From this point of view, Berger and others cannot lightly dismiss the activities of such men as LeRoi Jones who affirm soul and other black mystiques. Whether or not their every statement is judicious and wise, these spokesmen have a historic hand at present in the development of black culture. They know "where it's at", and they are there where the action is, and they influence this cultural action process because Negro culture is not a finished, a determined or a static thing.

The same is true for the notion of soul which Berger feels is becoming a stereotype. This does not tell us anything about its present or future significance. The cultural reality of an affirmed trait is not in its statistical or scientific reality but in what it does and accomplishes as a rallying point and symbol. As we have come to know unhappily in less ambiguous race-relations situations, stereotypes have living effects whatever the scientist may do to deflate them. The fate, function and thus reality of soul—like black power—remains to be revealed in the practical course of events. What soul is and becomes is therefore in part a product of the conscious decisions and political-educational activities of the cultural leadership of the Negro community and even more of the response of its less articulate masses. Its fate will not be determined by white social analysts like Keil, Berger or myself.

Whites are no longer calling the shots on these matters that most deeply affect black Americans. This is the great and historic gain of the last decade of Negro protest, culminating in the black-power mood—which from this viewpoint is not as total a departure from the previous civil rights activity as most people assume. And this applies also to the intellectual and social-science community's grappling with such issues as Negro culture. Yet even while our academic theorizing is no longer as central as it once may have been, the Negro political and cultural movement still operates within these American conditions that we affect. For this reason, white social scientists have a responsibility to probe deeply into the assumptions and consequences of our characterizations of race relations in this country. This I believe justifies the present essay which concludes with a consideration of the neoracist under-pinning and consequences of the "no Negro culture" thesis.

If the task of the white liberal and radical is to elimi-nate racism from the body politic, the parallel task of the white intellectual in the struggle for a democratic society is to expose and combat racism in the spheres of ideology and culture. When racism was primarily empressed in its classical form, this was a relatively simple task since the prime ideological targets were the traditional stereotypes: the various beliefs in racial inferiority and related notions that Myrdal so well dissects in *An American Dilemma*. Liberal social scientists like Thomas Pettigrew have con-tinued this task with respect to such present day issues as intelligence and crime. But today conventional racist beliefs are no longer legitimate; they have existed longer among the less-educated masses but have already lost out in the ideological struggle among the cultured and the en-lightened. Here however, they have been replaced with the new academic and liberal assumptions that are on the surface democratic ideas. It is these beliefs and practices that I have termed *neoracism*.

Neoracism is not easy to define because the attitudes that make up this complex are extremely subtle. They are liberal beliefs in that they usually reflect more of a positive, accepting attitude toward the colored group or individual than a negative, hostile one. The neoracist character of the idea generally stems not so much from its contents, but from the context in which the idea is applied. The racism involved is then usually the failure to take into account critical aspects of the situation, rather than the commission of an act or an adverse statement. Neoracism is commonplace, it is difficult to avoid because its absence requires postures and attitudes that straddle a most delicate balance between two polar positions—one of which usually appears

Tokenism and patronization are the more obvious forms of neoracism. They reflect the "see how much we've done" attitude or the "spades is in" attitude. The implicit neoracism involved is the denial or the minimization of the persistence of serious racial discrimination and the concern for the unusual or "qualified" Negro at the expense of the bulk of the group. Where conventional racism is expressed in brutalities (lynching, police harassment) and in outright exclusion, neoracism "includes" black people only when they meet standards that are not applied to whites. Thus liberal corporations recruit "Ivy League" Negroes who are good-looking and well-mannered, rejecting others who might be equally or more capable. Of greater importance are lingering unconscious attitudes that expect a limited "place" for the black man. The liberal organization partially integrates its force, but cannot handle a Negro man who is assertive and aggressive. Subtle pressures are exerted to contain him within a passive, quiescent mold that goes far beyond the general "organization man" constraints. The problems of competition between black and white in America are not all problems of the Negro.

Another form is the failure to make special efforts to change institutions so that their doors are in fact open and are seen as open. One neoracist extreme thus ignores the black American and his special problems on the assumption that group and color distinctions are irrelevant; at the opposite extreme is an attitude of over-concern, the over-befriending of minority persons. The nonracist stance is somewhere in that delicate middle area between respect for group values and individual uniqueness, a balance that varies with every situation.

Similar pitfalls exist in the ideal realm. A common liberal form of neoracism is the emphasis on the pathological features of Afro-American life. The strengths and positive virtues in this subculture are as much a part of the reality but they are usually minimized by social scientists who operate from the assumption of social and economic determinism, and tend to ignore the creative aspects of group life and history. At the same time the neglect of hardship and negative aspects of community structure leads to a romanticism at the other neoracist extreme. The intellectual transcendence of racism therefore requires a continual awareness of its power, persistence and causality without falling into the deterministic theory that it totally destroys human freedom and dignity.

The viewpoint that black culture is only a lower-class life-style and Negro Americans have no ethnic traditions to value and defend falls within this neoracist outlook. Superficially this argument seems to say that blacks are as American as whites and therefore, their cultural orientations reflect their social class position. But as I have pointed out this theory ignores the group-forming and culture producing effects of racism and therefore, as an analytical position leads to the minimization of the reality of racial oppression. In addition, this position leads to an over-concern with the pathological features of the black community at the expense of its unique strengths and contributions, since the culture of poverty is generally (and correctly) seen in terms of the predominance of suffering and the destruction of choice and human possibility. If Negro culture is only lower-class culture, then the questionable assumption that *all* black people want integration, mobility and assimilation (middle-class status) seems justifiable as a basis for institutional policy and it is not necessary to consult, to offer alternative choices or to respect individual diversity. Furthermore, this position is historically tied to past patterns of negating or appropriating the cultural possessions and productions of black people. The racist patterns was to destroy culture, to steal it for a profit or to view it contemptuously or with amusement. The neoracist equivalents today are to deny that any Negro culture exists or to envy and desire these values which the black man creates and defends as his own. (Witness the pathetic need of many young and not-so-young liberal and radical "friends" of the Negro movement to feel that they, too, have "soul".) The denial of Negro ethnicity is the more serious form that white appropriation takes today. Through abstract and intellectual analysis, the social scientist attempts to undermine the claims of Afro-Americans to a distinctive ethos and value-system. The very existence of our possibility to so influence the black cultural process is based on the original alienation of the black man from his African traditions. Because colored Americans could only use the English language to carry on their business, their politics and their intellectual life, their physical and moral communities became vulnerable to the penetration of white Americans in a way that other ethnic groups—insulated by exotic languages, religions and other institutions—could escape. Thus, the original culture-stripping and the consequent appropriation of indigenous black culture laid open the Negro community to economic and political colonialism, to the contamination of group ideology by alien, pride-destroying perspectives, and to the participation of paternalistic whites in racial movements. It is time for us to get out of the way and permit the black community to define for itself its relationship to American culture and society.

*Another *Look
*At *Lower-class *Black Culture

ULF HANNERZ

Some 5.7 million people were simply not counted in the 1960 census, and most of them, it now appears, were Negro men living in northern cities. This statistical oversight, if that is what it was, is not unique to the government's census takers. Ever since the beginnings of the scholarly study of black people in the Americas, there has been an interesting fascination with the differences between the family life of Negroes and that of their white counterparts, the chief difference being seen as the dominant, not to say dominating, role of women in black families.

From E. Franklin Frazier's pioneering 1932 study of *The Negro Family in Chicago* through Melville Herskovits' *The Myth of the Negro Past* in 1941 to the so-called Moynihan Report of 1965, social scientists have been repeatedly rediscovering, analyzing and worrying over the crucial role of the mother (or grandmother) in the family structure of blacks in the New World. Herskovits saw the cen-

167

trality of the mother as an African vestige, typical of the polygynous marriage in which every woman, with her off-spring, formed a separate unit. Frazier is generally regarded as the first to ascribe to the institution of slavery itself the strongest influence in undermining the stability of marriage, an influence that was later reinforced when blacks encountered what Frazier perceived as the peculiarly urban evils of anonymity, disorganization and the lack of social support and controls. Moynihan, like Frazier, sees the matriarchal family as being practically without strengths, at least in the context of the larger American society, but his Report emphasizes the ways in which employer discrimination and, more recently, welfare policies have contributed to the breaking up (or foreclosure) of the male-dominated family unit among blacks.

In all of these studies, however, the black *man*—as son, lover, husband, father, grandfather—is a distant and shadowy figure "out there somewhere" . . . if only because his major characteristic as far as the household is concerned is his marginality or absence.

I do not mean to suggest that the black man is undis-covered territory. Obviously he is not. His popular image was fixed for one (long) era in *Uncle Tom's Cabin* and prophetically fashioned for our own time in Norman Mailer's essay "The White Negro." Here is Mailer's Hipster, modeled on the Negro: "Sharing a collective disbelief in the words of men who had too much money and controlled too many things, they knew almost as powerful a disbelief in the socially monolithic ideas of the single mate, the solid family and the respectable love life." And here is Mailer's black man:

Knowing in the cells of his existence that life was war, nothing but war, the Negro (all exceptions admitted) could rarely afford the sophisticated inhibitions of civilization, and so he kept for his survival the art of the primitive, he lived in the enormous present, he subsisted for his Saturday night kicks, relinquishing the pleasures of the mind for the more obligatory pleasures of the body, and in his music he gave voice to the character and quality of his existence, to his rage and the infinite variations of joy, lust, languor, growl, cramp, pinch, scream and despair of his orgasm.

Certainly there is poetic exaggeration in Mailer's description, and perhaps a conscious effort to mythicize his subject; and certainly too there is a great deal of stereotyping in the general public's imagery of the people of the black ghetto. But hardly anyone acquainted with life in the ghetto can fail to see that Mailer's portrait captures much of the reality as well. Lee Rainwater's sketch of the "expressive life-style" of the black male shows a trained social scientist's analysis that is remarkably similar to Mailer's. And undoubtedly there *is* a sizable segment of the black male population that is strongly concerned with sex, drinking, sharp clothes and "trouble"; and among these men one finds many of those who are only marginally involved with married life. Of course, ghetto life styles are heterogeneous, and there are many men who live according to "mainstream" values; but it is to the ones who do not that we should turn our attention if we want to understand what kinds of masculinity go with the female-dominated family.

This essay is an attempt to outline the social processes within the ghetto communities of the northern United States whereby the identity of street-corner males is established and maintained. To set the stage and state the issues involved in this essay, I'd like to look at the views of two other observers of the ghetto male. One is Charles Keil, whose *Urban Blues* (1966) is a study of the bluesman as a "culture hero." According to Keil, the urban blues singer, with his emphasis on sexuality, "trouble" and flashy clothes, manifests a cultural model of maleness that is highly valued by ghetto dwellers and relatively independent of the mainstream cultural tradition. Keil criticizes a number of authors who, without cavilling at this description of the male role, tend to see it as rooted in the individual's anxiety about his masculinity. This, Keil finds, is unacceptably ethnocentric:

> Any sound analysis of Negro masculinity should first deal with the statements and responses of Negro women, the conscious motives of the men themselves and the Negro cultural tradition. Applied in this setting, psychological theory may then be able to provide important new insights in place of basic and unfortunate distortions.

Keil, then, comes out clearly for a cultural interpretation of the male role we are interested in here. But Elliot Liebow in *Tally's Corner* (1967), a study resulting from the author's participation in a research project that definitely considered ghetto life more in terms of social problems than as a culture, reaches conclusions which, in some of their most succint formulations, quite clearly contradict Keil's:

> Similarities between the lower-class Negro father and son ... do not result from "cultural transmission" but from the fact that the son goes out and independently experiences the same failures, in the same areas, and for much the same reasons as his father.

Thus father and son are "independently produced lookalikes." With this goes the view that the emphasis on sexual ability, drinking and so forth is a set of compensatory self-deceptions which can only unsuccessfully veil the street-corner male's awareness of his failure.

Keil and Liebow, as reviewed here, may be taken as representatives of two significantly different opinions on why black people in the ghettos, and in particular the males, behave differently than other Americans. One emphasizes a cultural determinism internal to the ghetto, the other an economic determinism in the relationship between the ghetto and the wider society. It is easy to see how the two views relate to one's perspective on the determinants of the domestic structure of ghetto dwellers. And it is also easy to see how these perspectives have considerable bearing on public policy, especially if it is believed that the ghetto family structure somehow prevents full participation by its members in the larger American society and economy. If it is held, for example, that broad social and economic factors, and particularly poverty, make ghetto families the way they are—and this seems to be the majority opinion among social scientists concerned with this area—then public policy should concentrate on mitigating or removing those elements that distort the lives of black people. But if the style of life in the ghetto is culturally determined and more or less independent of other "outside" factors, then public policy will have to take a different course, or drop the problem altogether *qua* problem.

Admittedly, the present opportunity structure places serious obstacles in the way of many ghetto dwellers, making a mainstream life-style difficult to accomplish. And if research is to influence public policy, it is particularly important to point to the wider structural influences that *can* be changed in order to give equal opportunity to ghetto dwellers. Yet some of the studies emphasizing such macrostructural determinants have resulted in somewhat crude conceptualizations that are hardly warranted by the facts and which in the light of anthropological theory appear very oversimplified.

First of all, let us dispose of some of the apparent opposition between the two points of view represented by Keil and Liebow. There is not necessarily any direct conflict between ecological-economic and cultural explanations; the tendency to create such a conflict in much of the current literature on poverty involves a false dichotomy. In anthropology, it is a commonplace that culture is usually both inherited and influenced by the community's relationship to its environment. Economic determination and cultural determinism can go hand in hand in a stable environment. Since the ecological niche of ghetto dwellers has long remained relatively unchanged, there seems to be no reason why their adaptation should not have become in some ways cultural. It is possible, of course, that the first stage in the evolution of the specifically ghetto life-style consisted of a multiplicity of identical but largely independent adaptations from the existing cultural background—mainstream or otherwise—to the given opportunity structure, as Liebow suggests. But the second stage of adaptation—involves a perception of the first-stage adaptation as a normal condition, a state of affairs which from then on can be expected. What was at first independent adaptation becomes transformed into a ghetto heritage of assumptions about the nature of man and society.

Yet Liebow implies that father and son are independently produced as streetcorner men, and that transmission of a ghetto-specific culture has a negligible influence. To those adhering to this belief, strong evidence in its favor is seen in the fact that ghetto dwellers—both men and women— often express conventional sentiments about sex and other matters. Most ghetto dwellers would certainly agree, at times at least, that education is a good thing, that gambling and drinking are bad, if not sinful, and that a man and a woman should be true to each other. Finding such opinions, and heeding Keil's admonition to listen to the statements and responses of the black people themselves, one may be led to doubt that there is much of a specific ghetto culture. But then, after having observed behavior among these same people that often and clearly contradicts their stated values, one has to ask two questions: Is there any reason to believe that ghetto-specific behavior is cultural? And, if it *is* cultural, what is the nature of the coexistence of mainstream culture and ghetto-specific culture in the black ghetto?

To answer the first question, one might look at the kinds of communications that are passed around in the ghetto relating to notions of maleness. One set of relationships in which such communications occur frequently is the family; another is the male peer group.

Much has been made of the notion that young boys in the ghetto, growing up in matrifocal households, are somehow deficient in or uncertain about their masculinity, because their fathers are absent or peripheral in household affairs. It is said that they lack the role models necessary for learning male behavior; there is a lack of the kind of information about the nature of masculinity which a father would transmit unintentionally merely by going about his life at home. The boys therefore supposedly experience a great deal of sex-role anxiety as a result of this cultural vacuum. It is possible that such a view contains more than a grain of truth in the case of some quite isolated female-headed households. Generally speaking, however, there may be less to it than meets the eye. First of all, a female-headed household without an adult male in residence but where young children are growing up—and where, therefore, it is likely that the mother is still rather young—is seldom one where adult males are totally absent. More or less steady boyfriends (sometimes including the separated father) go in and out. Even if these men do not assume a central household role, the boys can obviously use them as source material for the identification of male behavior. To be sure, the model is not a conventional middle-class one, but it still shows what males are like.

Furthermore, men are not the only ones who teach boys
about masculinity. Although role-modeling is probably essential, other social processes can contribute to identity formation. Mothers, grandmothers, aunts and sisters who have
observed men at close range have formed expectations about
the typical behavior of men which they express and which
influence the boys in the household. The boys will come to
share in the women's imagery of men, and often they will
find that men who are not regarded as good household
partners (that is, "good" in the conventional sense) are
still held to be attractive company. Thus the view is easily
imparted that the hard men, good talkers, clothes-horses
and all, are not altogether unsuccessful as men. The women
also act more directly toward the boys in these terms—
they have expectations of what men will do, and whether
they wish the boys to live up (or down) to the expectations, they instruct them in the model. Boys are advised not
to "mess with" girls, but at the same time it is emphasized
that messing around is the natural thing they will otherwise go out and do—and when the boys start their early
adventures with the other sex, the older women may scold
them but at the same time point out, not without satisfaction, that "boys will be boys." This kind of maternal
(or at least adult female) instruction of young males is
obviously a kind of altercasting, or more exactly, socialization to an alter role—that is, women cast boys in the role
complementary to their own according to their experience
of man-woman relationships. One single mother of three
boys and two girls put it this way:

> You know, you just got to act a little bit tougher with
> boys than with girls, 'cause they just ain't the same. Girls
> do what you tell them to do and don't get into no
> trouble, but you just can't be sure about the boys. I
> mean, you think they're OK and next thing you find

out they're playing hookey and drinking wine and maybe stealing things from cars and what not. There's just something bad about boys here, you know. But what can you say when many of them are just like their daddies? That's the man in them coming out. You can't really fight it, you know that's the way it is. They know, too, But you just got to be tougher.

This is in some ways an antagonistic socialization, but it is built upon an expectation that it would be unnatural for men not to turn out to be in some ways bad—that is fighters, drinkers, lady killers and so forth. There is one thing worse than a no-good man—the sissy, who is his opposite. A boy who seems weak is often reprimanded and ridiculed not only by his peers but also by adults, including his mother and older sisters. The combination of role-modeling by peripheral fathers or temporary boy-friends with altercasting by adult women certainly provides for a measure of male role socialization within the family.

And yet, when I said that the view of the lack of models in the family was too narrow, I was not referring to the observers' lack of insight into many matrifocal ghetto families as much as I was to the emphasis they placed on the family as *the* information storage unit of a community's culture. I believe it is an ethnocentrism on the part of middle-class commentators to take it for granted that if information about sex roles is not transmitted from father to son within the family, it is not transmitted from generation to generation at all. In American sociology, no less than in the popular mind, there is what Ray Birdwhistell has termed a "sentimental model" of family life, according to which the family is an inward-turning isolated unit, meeting most of the needs of its members, and certainly their needs for sociability and affection. The "sentimental model" is hardly ever realistic even as far as middle-class Amer-

ican families are concerned, and it has even less relevance
for black ghetto life. Ghetto children live and learn out on
the streets just about as much as within the confines of the
home. Even if mothers, aunts and sisters do not have streetcorner men as partners, there is an ample supply of them
on the front stoop or down at the corner. Many of these
men have such a regular attendance record as to become
quite familiar to children and are frequently very friendly
with them. Again, therefore, there is no lack of adult men
to show a young boy what men are like. It seems rather un-
likely that one can deny all role-modeling effect of these
men on their young neighbors. They may be missing in the
United States census records, but they are not missing in
the ghetto community.

Much of the information gained about sex roles outside
the family comes not from adult to child, however, but
from persons in the same age-grade or only slightly higher.
The idea of culture being stored in lower age-grades must
be taken seriously. Many ghetto children start participating
in the peer groups of the neighborhood at an early age,
often under the watchful eye of an elder brother or sister.
In this way they are initiated into the culture of the peer
group by interacting with children—predominantly of the
same sex—who are only a little older than they are. And
in the peer-group culture of the boys, the male sex role is a
fairly constant topic of concern. Some observers have felt
that this is another consequence of the alleged sex role
anxiety of ghetto boys. This may be true, of course, at
least in that it may have had an important part in the development of male peer-group life as a dominant element
of ghetto social structure. Today, however, such a simple
psychosocial explanation will not do. Most ghetto boys
can hardly avoid associating with other boys, and once they
are in the group, they are efficiently socialized into a high

degree of concern with their sex role. Much of the joking, the verbal contests and the more or less obscene songs among small ghetto boys, serve to alienate them from dependence on mother figures and train them to the exploitative, somewhat antagonistic attitude toward women which is typical of streetcorner men.

This is not to say that the cultural messages are always very neat and clear-cut. In the case of the kind of insult contest called "playing the dozens," "sounding" or (in Washington, D. C.) "joning," a form of ritualized interaction which is particularly common among boys in the early teens, the communication is highly ambiguous. When one boy says something unfavorable about another's mother, the other boy is expected either to answer in kind or to fight in defense of his honor (on which apparently that of his mother reflects). But the lasting impression is that there is something wrong about mothers—they are not as good as they ought to be ("Anybody can get pussy from your mother"), they take over male items of behavior and by implication too much of the male role ("Your mother smokes a pipe"). If standing up for one's family is the manifest expected consequence of "the dozens," then a latent function is a strengthening of the belief that ghetto women are not what they ought to be. The other point of significance is that the criteria of judgment about what a good woman should be like are apparently like those of the larger society. She should not be promiscuous, and she should stick to the mainstream female role and not be too dominant.

The boys, then, are learning and strengthening a cultural ambivalence involving contradictions between ideal and reality in female behavior. I will return to a discussion of such cultural ambivalence later. But the point remains that even this game involves continuous learning and strengthening of a cultural definition of what women are like that is in some ways complementary to the definition of what men are like. And much of the songs, the talk and the action—fighting, sneaking away with girls into a park or an alley or drinking out of half-empty wine bottles stolen from or given away by adult men—are quite clearly preparations for the streetcorner male role. If boys and men show anxiety about their masculinity, one may suspect that this is induced as much by existing cultural standards as by the alleged nonexistence of models.

This socialization within the male peer group is a continuing process; the talk that goes on, continuously or intermittently, at the street corner or on the front steps may deal occasionally with a football game or a human-interest story from the afternoon newspaper, but more often there are tales from personal experience about adventures of drinking (often involving the police), about women won and lost, about feminine fickleness and the masculine guile (which sometimes triumphs over it), about clothing, or there may simply be comments on the women passing down the street. "Hi ugly . . . don't try to swing what you ain't got."

This sociability among the men seems to be a culture-building process. Shared definitions of reality are created out of the selected experiences of the participants. Women are nagging and hypocritical; you can't expect a union with one of them to last forever. Men are dogs; they have to run after many women. There is something about being a man and drinking liquor; booze makes hair grow on your chest. The regularity with which the same topics appear in conversation indicates that they have been established as the expected and appropriate subjects in this situation, to the exclusion of other topics.

■ Mack asked me did I screw his daughter, so I asked:

"I don't know, what's her name?" And then when I heard that gal was his daughter all right, I says, "Well, Mack, I didn't really have to take it. 'cause it was given to me." I thought Mack sounded like his daughter was some goddam white gal. But Mack says, "Well, I just wanted to hear it from you." Of course, I didn't know that was Mack's gal, 'cause she was married and had a kid, and so she had a different name. But then you know the day after when I was out there a car drove by, and somebody called my name from it, you know, "hi darling," and that was her right there. So the fellow I was with says, "Watch out, Buddy will shoot your ass off." Buddy, that's her husband. So I says, "Yeah, but he got to find me first!"

■ Let me tell you fellows, I've been arrested for drunkenness more than two hundred times over the last few years, and I've used every name in the book. I remember once I told them I was Jasper Gonzales, and then I forgot what I had told them, you know. So I was sitting there waiting, and they came in and called "Jasper Gonzales," and nobody answered. I had forgotten that's what I said, and to tell you the truth, I didn't know how to spell it. So anyway, nobody answered, and there they were calling "Jasper Gonzales. Jasper Gonzales!" So I thought that must be me, so I answered. But they had been calling a lot of times before that. So the judge said, "Mr. Gonzales, are you of Spanish descent?" And I said, "Yes, your honor, I came to this country thirty-four years ago." And of course I was only thirty-five, but you see I had this beard then, and I looked pretty bad, dirty and everything, you know, so I looked like sixty. And so he said, "We don't have a record on you. This is the first time you have been arrested?" So I said, "Yes, your honor, nothing like this happened to me before. But my wife was sick, and then I lost my job you know, and I felt kind of bad. But it's the first time I ever got drunk." So he said, "Well, Mr. Gonzales, I'll let you go, 'cause you are not like the rest of them here. But let this be a warning to you." So I said, "Yes, your honor." And then I went out, and so I said to myself, "I'll have to celebrate this." So I went across the street from the court, and you know there are four liquor stores there, and I got a pint of wine and next thing I was drunk as a pig.

■ Were you here that time a couple of weeks ago when these three chicks from North Carolina were up here visiting Miss Gladys? They were really gorgeous, about 30-35. So Charlie says why don't we step by the house and he and Jimmy and Deekay can go out and buy them a drink. So they say they have to go and see this cousin first, but then they'll be back. But then Brenda (Charlie's wife) comes back before they do, and so these girls walk back and forth in front of the house, and Charlie can't do a thing about it, except hope they won't knock on his door. And then Jimmy and Deekay come and pick them up, and Fats is also there, and the three of them go off with these chicks, and there is Charlie looking through his window, and there is Brenda looking at them too, and asking Charlie does he know who the chicks are.

Groups of one's friends give some stability and social sanction to the meanings that streetcorner men attach to their experiences—meanings that may themselves have been learned in the same or preceding peer groups. They, probably more than families, are information storage units for the ghetto-specific male role. At the same time, they are self-perpetuating because they provide the most satisfactory contexts for legitimizing the realities involved. In other words, they suggest a program for maleness, but they also offer a haven of understanding for those who follow that program and are criticized for it or feel doubts about it. For of course all streetcorner males are more or less constantly exposed to the definitions and values of the mainstream cultural apparatus, and so some cultural ambivalence can hardly be avoided. Thus, if a man is a dog for running after women—as he is often said to be among ghetto dwellers—he wants to talk about it with other dogs who appreciate that this is a fact of life. If it is natural for men to drink, let it happen among other people who understand the nature of masculinity. In this way the group maintains constructions of reality, and life according to this reality maintains the group.

It is hard to avoid the conclusion, then, that there is a cultural element involved in the sex roles of streetcorner males, because expectations about sex are manifestly shared and transmitted rather than individually evolved. (If the latter had been the case, of course, it would have been less accurate to speak of these as roles, since roles are by definition cultural.) This takes us to the second question stated above, about the coexistence of conventional and ghetto-specific cultures. Streetcorner men certainly are aware of the male ideal of mainstream America—providing well for one's family, remaining faithful to one's spouse, staying out of trouble, etc.—and now and then everyone of them states it as his own ideal. What we find here, then, may be seen as a bicultural situation. Mainstream culture and ghetto-specific culture provide different models for living, models familiar to everyone in the ghetto. Actual behavior may lean more toward one model or more toward the other, or it may be some kind of mixture, at one point or over time. The ghetto-specific culture, including the streetcorner male role, is adapted to the situation and the experience of the ghetto dweller; it tends to involve relatively little idealization but offers shared expectations concerning self, others and the environment. The mainstream culture, from the ghetto dweller's point of view, often involves idealization, but there is less real expectation that life will actually follow the paths suggested by those ideals. This is not to say that the ghetto-specific culture offers no values of its own at all, or that nothing of mainstream culture ever appears realistic in the ghetto; but in those areas of life where the two cultures exist side by side as alternative guides to action (for naturally, the ghetto-specific culture, as distinct from mainstream culture, is not a "complete" culture covering all areas of life), the ghetto-specific culture is often taken to forecast what one can actually expect from life, while the mainstream norms are held up as perhaps ultimately more valid but less attainable under the given situational constraints. "Sure it would be good to have a good job and a good home and your kids in college and all that, but you got to be yourself and do what you know." Of course, this often makes the ghetto-specific cultural expectations into self-fulfilling prophecies, as ghetto dwellers try to attain what they believe they can attain; but, to be sure, self-fulfilling prophecies and realistic assessments may well coincide.

On the whole, one may say that both mainstream culture and ghetto-specific culture are transmitted within many ghetto families. I have noted how socialization into the ghetto male role within the household is largely an informal process, in which young boys may pick up bits and pieces of information about masculinity from the women in the house as well as from males who may make their entrances and exits. On the other hand, when adult women —usually mothers or grandmothers—really "tell the boys how to behave," they often try to instill in them main-stream, not to say puritanical norms—drinking is bad, sex is dirty and so forth. The male peer groups, as we have seen, are the strongholds of streetcorner maleness, although there are times when men cuss each other out for being "no good." Finally, of course, mainstream culture is trans-mitted in contacts with the outside world, such as in school or through the mass media. It should be added, though, that the latter may be used selectively to strengthen some elements of the streetcorner male role; ghetto men are drawn to Westerns, war movies and crime stories both in the movie house and on their TV sets.

Yet, even if the nature of men's allegiance to the two cultures makes it reasonably possible to adhere, after a fashion, to both at the same time, the bicultural situation of streetcorner males involves some ambivalence. The re-jection of mainstream culture as a guide to action rather than only a lofty ideal is usually less than complete. Of course, acting according to one or the other of the two cultures to a great extent involves bowing to the demands of the social context, and so a man whose concerns in the peer-group milieu are drinking and philandering will try to be "good" in the company of his mother or his wife and children, even if a complete switch is hard to bring about. There are also peer groups, of course, that are more mainstream-oriented than others, although even the mem-bers of these groups are affected by streetcorner definitions of maleness. To some extent, then, the varying allegiance of different peer groups to the two cultures is largely a difference of degree, as the following statement by a young man implies.

Those fellows down at the corner there just keep drink-ing and drinking. You know, I think it's pretty natural for a man to drink, but they don't try to do nothing about it, they just drink every hour of the day, every day of the week. My crowd, we drink during the weekend, but we can be on our jobs again when Monday comes.

However, although where one is or who one is with does bring some order into this picture of bicultural ambivalence, it is still one of less than perfect stability. The drift between contexts is itself not something to which men are committed by demands somehow inherent in the social structure. Ghetto men may spend more time with the family, or more time with the peer group, and the extent to which they choose one or the other, and make a concomitant cultural selection, still appears to depend much on personal attachment to roles, and to changes in them. The social alignments of a few men may illustrate this. One man, Norman Hawkins, a construction laborer, spends practically all his leisure time at home with his family, only occasionally joining in the streetcorner conversations and behavior of the peer group to which his neighbor, Harry Jones, belongs. Harry Jones, also a construction worker, is also married and has a family but stays on the periphery of household life, although he lives with his wife and children. Some of the other men in the group are unmarried or separated and so seldom play the "family man" role which Harry Jones takes on now and then. Harry's younger brother, Carl, also with a family, used to participate intensively in peer group life until his drinking led to a serious ailment, and after he recuperated from this he started spending much less time with his male friends and more with his family. Bee Jay, a middle-aged bachelor who was raised by his grandmother, had a job at the post office and had little to do with street life until she died. Since then, he has become deeply involved with a tough, hard-drinking group and now suffers from chronic health prob-

lems connected with his alcoholism. Thus we can see how
the life careers of some ghetto men take them through
many and partly unpredictable shifts and drifts between
mainstream and ghetto-specific cultures, while others remain quite stable in one allegiance or another.

The sociocultural situation in the black ghetto is clearly
complicated. The community shows a great heterogeneity
of life-styles; individuals become committed in some degree to different ways of being by the impersonally-en-
forced structural arrangements to which they are subjected,
but unpredictable contingencies have an influence, and their
personal attachments to life-styles also vary. The socioeconomic conditions impose limits on the kinds of life
ghetto dwellers may have, but these kinds of life are culturally transmitted and shared as many individuals in the
present, and many in the past, live or have lived under
the same premises. When the latter is the case, it is hardly
possible to invent new adaptations again and again, as men
are always observing each other and interacting with each
other. The implication of some of Frazier's writings, that
ghetto dwellers create their way of life in a cultural limbo
—an idea which has had more modern expressions—appears
as unacceptable in this case as in any other situation where
people live together, and in particular where generations
live together. The behavior of the streetcorner male is a
natural pattern of masculinity with which ghetto dwellers
grow up and which to some extent they grow into. To see
it only as a complex of unsuccessful attempts at hiding
failures by self-deception seems, for many of the men involved, to be too much psychologizing and too little sociology. But this does not mean that the attachment to the
ghetto-specific culture is very strong among its bearers.

The question whether streetcorner males have mainstream culture or a specific ghetto culture, then, is best

answered by saying that they have both, in different ways. There can be little doubt that this is the understanding most in line with that contemporary trend in anthropological thought which emphasizes the sharing of cultural imagery, of expectations and definitions of reality, as the medium whereby individuals in a community interact. It is noteworthy that many of the commentators who have been most skeptical of the idea of a ghetto-specific culture, or more generally a "culture of poverty," have been those who have taken a more narrow view of culture as a set of values about which an older generation consciously instructs the younger ones in the community.

Obviously, the answer to whether there is a ghetto-specific culture or not will depend to some extent on what we shall mean by culture. Perhaps this is too important a question to be affected by a mere terminological quibble, and perhaps social policy, in some areas, may well proceed unaffected by the questions raised by a ghetto-specific culture. On the other hand, in an anthropological study of community life, the wider view of cultural sharing and transmission which has been used here will have to play a part in our picture of the ghetto, including that of what ghetto males are like.

October 1969

The study from which this article was adapted is scheduled for 1970 publication by The Free Press as a chapter of the forthcoming *Afro-American Anthropology: Contemporary Perspectives,* edited by Norman E. Whitten, Jr. and John F. Swed. All rights are reserved by the Free Press.